PAINTING & DECORATING CABINETS & CHESTS

PHILLIP C. MYER

NORTH LIGHT BOOKS
CINCINNATI, OHIO

A NOTE ABOUT SAFETY

Due to toxicity concerns, most art and craft material manufacturers have begun labeling their products with proper health warnings or nontoxic seals. It is always important to read a manufacturer's label when using a product for the first time. Follow any warnings about not using the product when pregnant or contemplating pregnancy, about keeping the product out of reach of children or about incompatible products. Always work in a well-ventilated room when using products with fumes.

The information in this book is presented in good faith, but no warranty is given, nor results guaranteed, nor is freedom from any patent to be inferred. Since we have no control over physical conditions surrounding the application of products, techniques and information herein, the publisher and author disclaim any liability for results.

Painting & Decorating Cabinets & Chests. Copyright © 1998 by Phillip C. Myer. Manufactured in Singapore. All rights reserved. No part of this book may be reproduced in any form or by any electronic or mechanical means including information storage and retrieval systems without permission in writing from the publisher, except by a reviewer, who may quote brief passages in a review. Published by North Light Books, an imprint of F&W Publications, Inc., 1507 Dana Avenue, Cincinnati, Ohio 45207. (800) 289-0963. First Edition.

Other fine North Light Books are available at your local bookstore or direct from the publisher.

02 01 00 99 98   5 4 3 2 1

Library of Congress Cataloging-in-Publication Data

Myer, Phillip C.
    Painting & decorating cabinets & chests / Phillip C. Myer.
        p.   cm.—(Creative finishes series)
    Includes index.
    ISBN 0-89134-804-2 (pbk.)
    1. Furniture painting. 2. Texture painting. 3. Cabinetwork. 4. Chests. 5. Decoration and ornament. I. Title. II. Series.
TT199.4.M944   1998
684.1′6—dc21   98-19914
                                                                      CIP

Edited by Chalice J. Bruce
Production edited by Michelle Howry
Cover design by Sandy Kent and Mary Barnes-Clark

Dedication

I would like to dedicate this book to the many students who have attended seminars and workshops with me over the past twenty years. A student's desire to grow and learn continues to inspire and motivate my art.

SPECIAL THANKS

Thanks and gratitude go to the individuals who have assisted with this book. Many thanks to the manufacturers and their representatives I have had the pleasure of working with: Dee Silver of Silver Brush Limited (Golden Natural and faux brush lines), Margo Christensen of Martin / F. Weber Co. (Prima Artist's Acrylics) and John McDonald of Back Street, Inc. (Faux Easy glazes). I would also like to thank the manufacturers and representatives who produce the ready-to-decorate chest and trunks featured in this book: Cabin Crafters; Valhalla Designs; Khoury, Inc.; Wayne's Woodenware; Mountain Man Products; Bush's Smoky Mt. Wood Products; Sechtem's Wood Products; The Cutting Edge; Unique Woods; Allen's Wood Crafts and Country Crafts by Dal.

ABOUT THE AUTHOR

Phillip C. Myer has been painting for more than twenty-five years. He is the author of *Creative Paint Finishes for the Home*, *Creative Paint Finishes for Furniture*, *Painting & Decorating Boxes*, *Painting & Decorating Tables* and *Painting & Decorating Frames* (North Light Books), as well as a dozen softcover books on tole and decorative painting. He has appeared in how-to decorating television segments on *Decorating with Style*, *Home Matters* and *Handmade by Design*. Phillip also has produced four instructional videos on painting and decorating techniques. A member of the Society of Decorative Painters for over twenty-two years, Phillip teaches seminars across the United States, Canada and Argentina, and at his Atlanta-based studios. Phillip and his business partner, Andy Jones, create custom-painted furniture and interior decorating through their business—PCM Studios.

TABLE OF CONTENTS

INTRODUCTION

It is often easy to overlook the decorative possibilities in utilitarian pieces such as cabinets and chests, so practical for storing clothing, food, stationery and sentimental treasures. But the broad, flat surfaces on these pieces offer the ideal opportunity to work a little painting and decorating magic. Cabinets and chests are like blank canvases waiting for your creativity to explode upon them with color, texture and pattern!

As you discover the range of techniques taught in this book—from folk, stroke and decorative painting styles to faux finishes to abstract effects—remember that you can easily change the pattern or color scheme to complement your home's decor. Choose colors or repeat a motif from a room's fabrics, wall coverings or rugs. Personalize what you create as much as possible. One of the main reasons to paint and decorate these surfaces is to make your pieces stand apart from mass-produced furniture.

Begin by painting and decorating old flea market or yard sale cabinets and chests. Then, once you've gained confidence and perfected these techniques, you might want to shop for your next projects at unfinished furniture stores or through mail order sources.

As I tell all my students, always keep an open mind. The decorating possibilities are boundless—you are only limited by your own creativity. Every time something doesn't go as planned, it might actually be a happy accident—and the start of a whole new level of artistic endeavor. Good luck and enjoy decorating your cabinets and chests. Maybe one day I will have the pleasure of sharing my decorating techniques with you firsthand in a seminar.

Phillip C. Myer

BEFORE YOU BEGIN

There are a few things to familiarize yourself with before beginning to decorate cabinets and chests. Knowledge and organization are key to your success with the techniques taught in this book. Take time to read the next few pages thoroughly; they review the general tools, basic techniques, and transfer, preparation, trimming and finishing methods. Although each project in this book is a self-contained unit, complete with a tools-and-materials list and illustrated, step-by-step instructions, the following foundation material will get you started on the right track.

PAINTS, GLAZES AND VARNISHES

The house paint, art material and craft supply industries have begun a strong movement toward developing and manufacturing environmentally friendly, water-based products. These products are nontoxic, have little or no odor and clean up easily with soap and water. The projects in this book are executed with a majority of these new-age, environmentally protective products.

Acrylic Paints

To create your own color mixtures in small quantities appropriate for painting cabinets and chests, a set of artist's grade or student grade acrylic paints in true artist's pigments will prove useful. I like working with Prima Acrylics. The following colors provide a good, basic palette for mixing a range of colors: Alizarin Crimson, Bright Red, Burnt Sienna, Burnt Umber, Cadmium Orange, Cadmium Red Light, Cadmium Yellow Light, Iridescent Gold, Iridescent White, Mars Black, Metallic Gold, Phthalo Green, Raw Umber, Titanium White and Ultramarine Blue.

Oil Paints

A few of the projects in this book were painted with artist's oil colors to achieve rich, transparent color and to take advantage of their long blending time. I've used Permalba oils and Prima oils in the following colors. Alizarin Crimson, Burnt Sienna, Burnt Umber, Cadmium Yellow Medium, Ice Blue, Leaf Green, Prussian Blue and Titanium White.

Latex-Based Paints

To provide a foundation for the paint and craft techniques, you'll need a selection of base paints; each project will specify either flat or semigloss latex-based paint. You can have these colors mixed at a hardware store or home improvement center. Today, most house paint departments offer computer color matching to match any reference material you bring them, such as fabric, wallpaper or carpet.

For the projects in this book, a quart or gallon of base paint, depending on the size of the piece, should suffice. For smaller amounts, look for 2-, 8- or 16-ounce squeeze bottles of acrylics at art and craft stores. These small sizes are great for trim colors on cabinets and chests. You won't be able to get custom color matches with these ready-made paints, but you'll pay less and waste less.

Acrylic Glazing Medium

Some of the projects require the use of a colored glaze. Create these colored glazes by adding artist's acrylic or latex house paint to a clear glazing medium. You can choose from the many ready-made, clear-glazing products on the market—or you can make your own by mixing equal amounts of water-based polyurethane varnish, acrylic retarder and water in a jar and stirring thoroughly.

Whichever type of clear glazing medium you choose, you'll want a glaze product that has a sufficient open time (working time) to allow you to manipulate the wet glaze and paint. Due to the size of most chest and trunk projects, you'll require at least fifteen to thirty minutes of open time to achieve successful results.

Ready-Made Colored Glazes

Ready-made, pretinted glazes require no mixing or measuring and are ready to use from the jar. I've used Anita's Faux Easy glazes for many of the colored glazes found in this book. There are twenty-four colors in the Faux Easy glaze collection, which can be mixed to create a range of custom colors.

Water-Based Varnishes

Water-based polyurethane varnishes are used in the techniques throughout this book. These varnishes, such as Anita's, provide durability, a broad open time, and greater water and alcohol resistance than standard acrylic water-based varnishes. To finish your cabinets and chests, you can choose a satin, semigloss or gloss varnish.

Spray Finishes

Today, there are several types of environment-friendly spray finishes. You can choose clear or colored acrylic-based sprays—in satin, semigloss or gloss sheen—to coat, seal and protect your decorated cabinets and chests.

BRUSHES

As you build your repertoire of techniques, you can also build your brush collection. There are several brushes—considered "workhorse" brushes—that are listed in just about every project's supply list. You'll use these brushes again and again, but with proper care they will last a long time. All the brushes listed here are manufactured by Silver Brush Limited.

Basecoat Bristle Brush

This is a 3-inch (7.5cm) brush made of natural hairs cut at a tapered angle to form a sharp, chisel edge. This

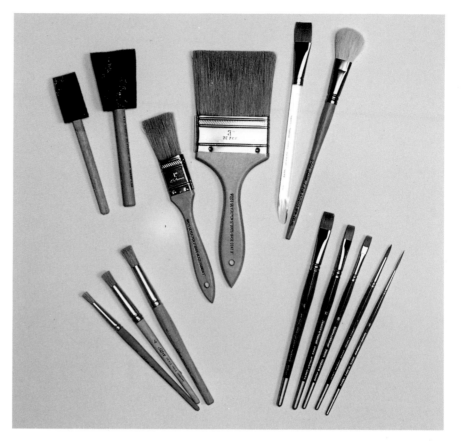

edge allows you to paint a straight line, control base-paint application, work the brush into tight spots and stroke on a smooth, even basecoat.

Glaze Brush

Available in widths of one and two inches (2.5cm and 5cm), the glaze brush is made from soft, natural hairs cut at a tapered angle. The natural hairs soak in a good amount of glaze and allow you to stroke a fair amount of glaze on the surface. Brushes with synthetic hairs do not provide this control because the artificial hair cannot drink in moisture.

Varnish Brush

Available in 1- and 2-inch (2.5cm and 5cm) sizes, this natural-hair brush allows you great control when applying a water-based varnish. The hairs drink in the varnish, then release it when pressure is applied to the brush. This size brush is also useful for get-

ting varnish into tight, recessed areas.

Silver Mop Brush

Made of soft, natural hairs, the ¾-inch (1.9cm) mop brush allows you to move and blend the paint with great ease and control. The small shape enables you to get into specific areas.

Golden Natural Flats

Flat shader brushes in nos. 4, 8, 12 and 16 provide a range of sizes to complete decorative painting and detail work. These brushes are made from a combination of natural and synthetic hairs. They have sharp chisel edges to access specific areas and to paint clean, sharp edges and lines.

Golden Natural Round

A no. 4 round brush provides the fine point needed for brushstrokes, detail and cleanup work. Made of natural and synthetic hairs, it will hold a good deal of paint.

Golden Natural Script Liner

A no. 2 script liner will provide crisp line work. This brush's hairs are about one-half to three-quarters of an inch (1.3cm to 1.9cm) longer than those of a standard liner brush, so they hold more paint and create a longer detail line.

Sponge Brushes

Polyfoam brushes (sponge brushes) in one- or two-inch (2.5cm or 5cm) widths are ideal for trim and some basecoat painting. They can also be used to apply glue. Do not use sponge brushes for varnish application because air bubbles will form; a natural-hair varnish brush provides better results.

Flogger Brush

This brush is made of a combination of natural and synthetic hairs that measure 5 inches (12.5cm) in length beyond the metal ferrule. This brush produces unique marks in the wet paint glaze. The long hairs can create strie, flogging and dragging techniques.

Blending Softener Brush

This brush is made from soft, natural goat hair. Available in 2- and 3-inch (5cm and 7.5cm) sizes, it is needed for fine blending techniques. The soft hairs of this style brush allow you to move paint and blend with great ease.

TOOLS

You'll need to gather an assortment of tools and materials to decorate the cabinets and chests in this book. These basic supplies will give you a creative tool box to use for future projects. Refer to the supply lists at the beginning of each technique to determine what you need for a specific project.

Tracing Paper

Transparent tracing paper in 12" × 16" (30cm × 41cm) pads or in rolls 24" (61cm) long will be used for tracing and drawing pattern designs.

Palette Knife and Paint Stirrers

A palette knife with a long, wide, flexible blade is required to thoroughly mix the paint and glaze mixtures. Wood paint stirrers are needed to mix quarts of paint.

Wax-Coated Palette and Foam Plates

A 12" × 16" (30cm × 41cm) wax-coated palette and flat foam plates (with no divided sections) can be used as surfaces for mixing small amounts of acrylic/latex paint and acrylic color glaze.

Metal Rulers

Rulers in 12- and 36-inch (30cm and 91cm) lengths with corked backings (to raise the edge above your work surface) will be used for measuring and ruling pen work.

Ruling Pen

A ruling pen can be filled with thinned paint to draw a fine trim or detail line. It has a slot area for holding paint and a turn screw to adjust the line width.

Craft Knife (X-Acto No. 11)

A craft knife with a sharp blade is ideal for cutting and scoring surfaces.

Brayer

A rubber brayer is used to roll over and smooth out surfaces. It is handy for pressing down sections of paper.

Credit Card

The hard plastic edge of a credit card can be used as a burnishing tool for rubbing down edges of tape when masking an area. The tip of a large metal spoon will provide similar results.

Tapes

Several types of tapes are required when painting. They should all be repositionable so you can pull up the tape without harming the coating below. The white Safe Release tape and blue Long Mask tape manufactured by 3M provide good edges for painting straight lines. Easy Mask's brown painter's tape is wider, providing broader coverage and protection, and it has adhesive along only one-half of the tape to minimize the risk of pulling up paint when you remove the tape.

Sandpaper

A variety of sandpaper in coarse (#60), medium (#100), fine (#150) and ultrafine (#400 and #600) grades will be required to smooth out or distress surfaces.

Miscellaneous Items

The following are some standard household and painting items. Many are considered tools or materials that "go without mentioning" when referring to basic methods in this book. For example, if you are using a quart of paint, you'll need something to open it with—a paint key.

- Acetone
- Acrylic retarder
- Bar soap
- Cheesecloth
- Clear acrylic spray
- Containers—small and large margarine tubs
- Cotton rags
- Craft glue
- Drop cloths
- Dry ballpoint pen or stylus
- Erasers
- Graphite transfer paper
- Hammer
- Murphy Oil Soap
- No-odor turpentine (Turpenoid)
- Paint key
- Paper sacks
- Paste wax
- Pencils
- Plastic gloves
- Putty knife
- Sanding block
- Spackling compound
- Steel wool—#0000
- Tack cloth
- Toothbrush
- White transfer paper
- Wood putty

THE BASICS

There are a few basic techniques that apply to most of the projects in this book. That's why it's a good idea to read the following information to prepare yourself for the painting adventures that lie ahead.

PRIMING AND PREPARING

Before the cabinets and chests are decorated with paint they require a coat of primer to seal surfaces and create a "tooth" for good adhesion. A white, stain-blocking primer, such as KILZ 2, provides a solid foundation on wood. Apply one or two coats, lightly sanding when dry.

BASECOATING

An important step in the process of decorating a cabinet or chest is applying a base paint to the surface. It is critical to achieve good, smooth, even coverage with this foundation color. Follow these easy tips for successful basecoating: Always load the basecoat bristle brush with plenty of paint, saturating the bristles with color, then lightly stroke the bristles across the side of the paint container. You only need to load the brush one or two inches from the chisel edge. Next, stroke color on the surface.

Tackle one side of the cabinet or chest at a time. Apply paint into all recessed trim areas first, then proceed to the larger, flat areas. Always use long, fluid strokes; short, choppy strokes make for a messy-looking basecoat and may be magnified when decorative treatments are placed over

them. Apply one coat and let it dry thoroughly, following the drying schedule on the paint label. If you do not allow proper curing (drying) time, the next coat can sag and cause curtaining. Lightly sand between coats with a piece of paper bag or fine sandpaper. Remove dust with a tack cloth and proceed with basecoating.

CLEANING BRUSHES

Once you have invested in good-quality brushes, it is important to take care of them. Water-based products dry fairly rapidly even when mixed with retarders. So when you are finished painting a section, place your brush in a container of water. When you're finished for the day, take your brushes to the sink and wash them thoroughly with Murphy Oil Soap and water. Rinse the brush and wash a second time to verify that all traces of color have been removed, including any paint at the base of the bristles near the metal ferrule. Shake off excess moisture and allow the brushes to dry thoroughly before storing.

If for some reason you've allowed acrylic to dry in the brush hairs, a small amount of acetone will work out some or all of the dried acrylic. However, the acetone may be harmful to certain types of brush hairs.

SIDE LOADING

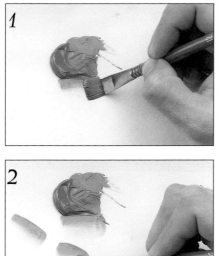

To side load a brush means to carry one color on one half of the brush. The paint is loaded so that it softly blends away on one side and leaves a crisp, defined line of color on the other. Begin by dipping your brush into the painting medium, blotting on a paper towel, and stroking one half of the brush along the pile of paint. On a clean area of your palette, use short pull strokes to blend the color into the medium until there's no discernible definition of where the color stops and the medium begins.

DOUBLE LOADING

A double-loaded brush carries two colors side by side with a smooth blend in between. You'll want to use a flat shader brush for this technique. Make two piles of paint mixed with medium to a thick, creamy consistency. Flatten the piles with a palette knife to form a clean, low edge to stroke up against. Begin by stroking both sides of one half of your brush through the lighter color paint. Now, stroke both sides of the other half of the brush along the darker color. On a clean area of your palette, use short pull strokes to blend the two colors together in the center of the brush. Restroke along each pile of paint and blend until the brush is saturated

PAT BLENDING

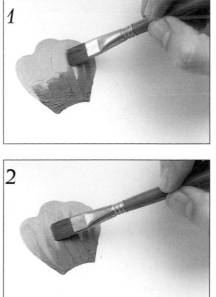

Pat blending softens one color into another while leaving visible brush marks. This technique is used for creating effects such as vein sections on leaves. Start by placing two colors side by side and doing some quick blending with your brush. Next, start at the darkest or lightest point and stroke a series of pull strokes, one overlapping another, to form streaks. You can keep these streaks consistent in width or make them gradually wider or narrower. You can make them straight or curve them to create movement. Continue pat blending from one color into another until you achieve a smooth transition.

COMMA STROKE

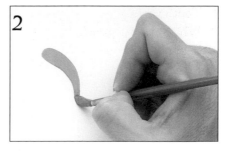

The comma stroke is the most recognizable brushstroke. It is also the most important brushstroke to master because it develops total brush control. Holding the loaded brush at an angle, touch it to the surface and apply pressure to form the head of the stroke. Curve the brush to the right or to the left, lifting it up to form the tail of the stroke. When using a round brush, twirl the brush slightly as you lift up, making a point with the bristles to form the tail. When using a flat shader brush, angle the brush upward, making a chisel edge to form the tail.

S-STROKE

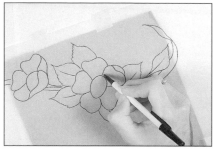

To form the S-stroke, load your brush with paint and, holding it an angle, draw a line stroke. Curve the brush to the right and apply pressure, dragging the brush to form a pull stroke. Begin to lift up on your brush, curving it to the left to form another line stroke at an angle. To create a backward S-stroke, reverse the direction of these strokes.

U-STROKE

To form the U-stroke, load your brush with paint, stand it on its tip and drag downward to form a line. As you reach the bottom, apply pressure while curving the brush upward. Lift the brush to form the upward line stroke.

TRACING AND TRANSFERRING

Some of these projects require the use of a pattern. You can use the patterns included in the back of this book or pick up designs elsewhere. You'll need to first use a copier to enlarge the design to fit your scale of cabinet or chest. For larger pieces, you may need to enlarge your first enlargements. Once the pattern is the correct size, cover the design with tracing paper and carefully trace the lines with a pencil or fine marker. To transfer the design to your cabinet or chest, tape the traced design in place with several pieces of tape. Depending on the background color, you'll slip either gray graphite paper (for light backgrounds) or white transfer paper (for dark backgrounds) under the traced design and go over the basic outline with a dried-out ballpoint pen or stylus. Lift up the tracing paper from time to time to see how well the design is transferring.

TRIMMING WITH A RULING PEN

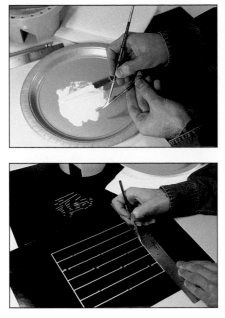

A ruling pen can create a fine line of color. Start by thinning the acrylic color with plenty of water; the paint mixture should be quite fluid but still have a little body to it. Next, load a round brush with thinned paint and stroke alongside the ruling pen's open slot to deposit the paint in the pen. Be sure to wipe away excess paint on the sides of the pen. Then, using a cork-backed, raised ruler (so paint does not seep under), hold the pen at a 45° angle and stroke alongside the ruler at a steady pace, allowing the paint to flow out in an even line. Complete all parallel lines first, let them dry, and then add perpendicular lines.

ANTIQUING

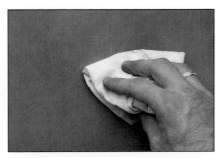

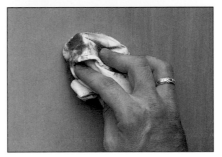

Many of the projects in this book have been tinted with a transparent color—or glaze. You can overglaze a surface in a multitude of colors. Antiquing implies the aging of a surface with darker, transparent glazes such as earth tones or black tones. When a lighter color is used to overglaze a surface, it's called highlighting.

To overglaze your cabinet or chest, you can use a ready-made color tinted glaze, or you can make your own. On small surfaces, you can simply thin paint with the appropriate medium—water for acrylic or latex paints, turpentine for oils. However, this mixture will not give you the time and control needed to overglaze larger cabinet and chest surfaces.

To make a clear, slow-drying glaze that will allow you to manipulate it, follow these recipes: If you are using water-based paints, mix a clear glaze of equal parts water-based polyurethane varnish, water and a liquid acrylic retarder. If you're working with oil paints, mix equal parts oil-based polyurethane varnish, turpentine and boiled linseed oil. Next, mix paint into the clear glaze until you achieve the desired transparent level of color. Test the color of your mixture by brushing it on a small area of your project and wiping off the desired amount.

Once your color-tinted glaze is prepared, use a glaze brush to apply it on one section of your project at a time. Using a cotton rag, start wiping off the glaze in a circular motion until you've achieved the desired level of color. Soften the coloring by lightly dusting the surface with a blending softener brush (for large areas) and a mop brush (for smaller areas).

If you like, you can finish this technique with flyspecking. Simply load a toothbrush with glaze and run your thumb or finger across the bristles to throw flecks of color onto the surface.

FINISHING

After you've decorated your cabinet or chest, you want to protect it. Use a natural-hair varnish brush to apply at least two coats of a water-based polyurethane varnish over the surface. Use a natural-hair varnish brush to flow on a coat of finish. Always be on the lookout for any varnish runs. Allow each coat to dry thoroughly before applying another coat.

For an elaborate, glass-like finish, apply a series of three coats of varnish (allowing the varnish to dry between coats). When the third coat is dry, wet the surface with water and soap, and rub the varnished surface in a circular motion with 400- or 600-grit sandpaper. (This technique is called wet sanding.) Wipe the surface with a clean paper towel. Apply three more coats of varnish, wet sand, and apply a final coat of varnish.

Faux Fabric: Red Plaid

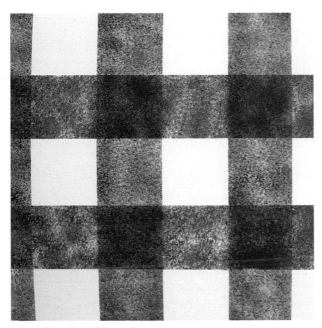

Detail from faux fabric chest.

This plaid fabric effect is simple to achieve with tape, paint and a brush. The secret to success is taking the time to properly measure and mark the placement of the color stripes. You can modify this example by adding thinner stripes in one or two coordinating colors. For example, the addition of blue and green stripes in both directions will create a tartan plaid effect. ❧

TOOLS AND
MATERIALS

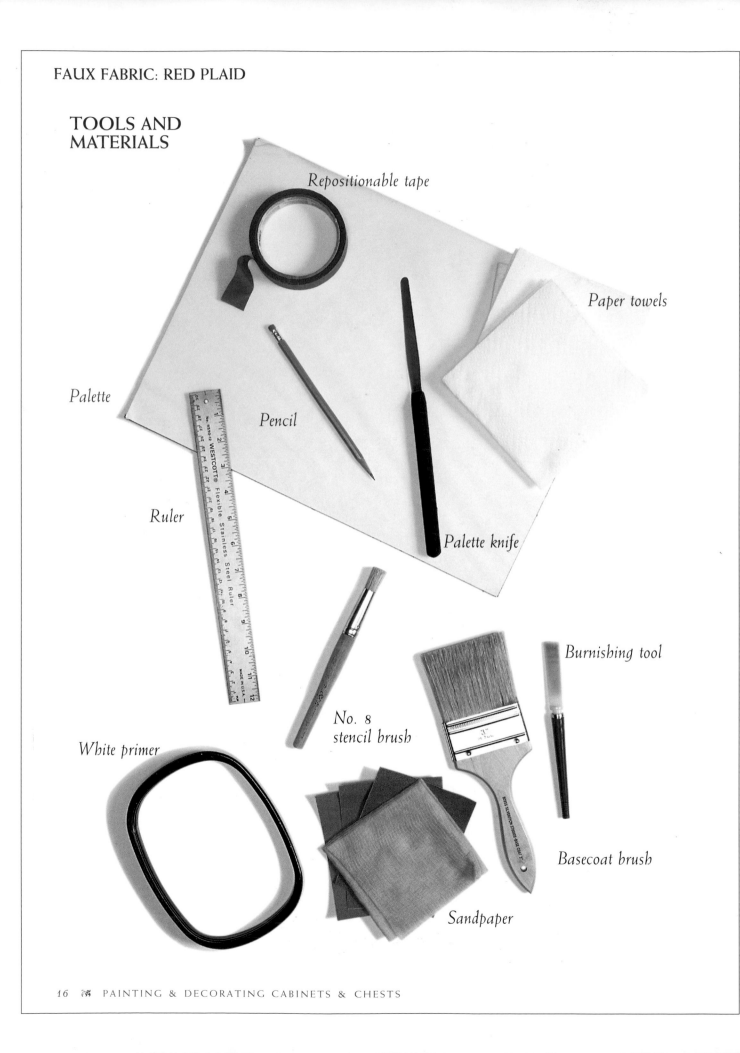

Repositionable tape

Paper towels

Palette

Pencil

Palette knife

Ruler

Burnishing tool

White primer

No. 8
stencil brush

Basecoat brush

Sandpaper

COLOR CHIPS—LATEX PAINT

White semigloss latex

Bright Red semigloss latex

1 Using a basecoat brush, prime the chest with white primer. Let the paint dry. Sand the surface and use a tack cloth to remove any sanding dust. Use the basecoat brush to base the chest in White semigloss latex paint. Apply several coats—allowing the paint to dry between coats—until an opaque coverage is achieved.

FAUX FABRIC: RED PLAID

2 To create stripes with crisp edges, use repositionable tape as a mask. First decide how wide you want to make the stripes of color. (In this example, they're the same width as the tape—1½ inches.) Next, use the ruler and pencil to measure and mark light guidelines for placing per-pendicular stripes on each side of the chest. Start by centering the first stripe in each direction and working out from there. Place tape on every other stripe in one direction, rubbing the edges down securely with a bur-nishing tool or your fingertip.

3 Load a stencil brush with Bright Red paint, dabbing on a paper towel to remove excess paint. You want a light dusting of paint on the brush's end bristles. In an up-and-down stippling motion, deposit a fairly even, dot-like pattern to the surface. Apply paint down all the taped-off stripes. Remove the tape by pulling it up slowly at a slight angle, watching for any lifting of basecoat color. Allow the paint to dry.

4 Once the first stripes are completely dry, place tape on every other stripe in the opposite direction. Rub the edges of the tape down well. Load the stencil brush with Bright Red paint, dabbing on a paper towel to remove excess paint, and stipple color down all the taped-off stripes.

5 After you've stippled all the stripes, carefully remove the tape. The intersecting areas have been stippled twice, creating the darker checks.

STROKE ART PAINTING: VINES AND BERRIES

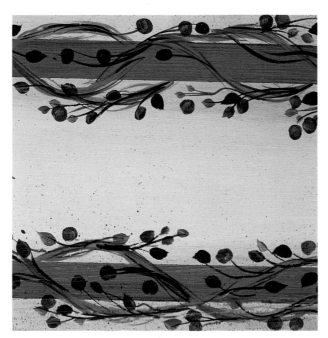

Detail from stroke art vine-and berry chest.

These vines and berries are painted in a very loose style using a simple stroke method. No blending, highlighting or shading is used to render individual form or the illusion of dimension. Ideal for achieving a casual, free-form look, this stroke art painting method can be adapted to subjects that have a flowing, linear quality such as ivy leaves or morning glories. 🍇

TOOLS AND MATERIALS

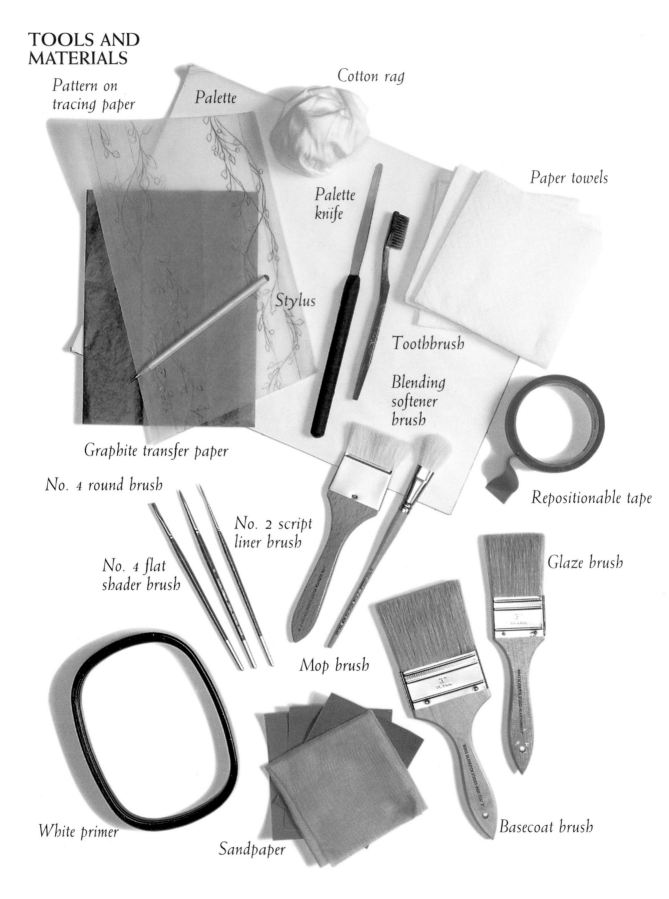

Pattern on
tracing paper

Palette

Cotton rag

Paper towels

Palette
knife

Stylus

Toothbrush

Blending
softener
brush

Graphite transfer paper

Repositionable tape

No. 4 round brush

No. 2 script
liner brush

No. 4 flat
shader brush

Glaze brush

Mop brush

White primer

Sandpaper

Basecoat brush

COLOR CHIPS—LATEX PAINT, ARTIST'S ACRYLICS

White semigloss latex
Pine Green semigloss latex
Alizarin Crimson
Alizarin Crimson plus
Burnt Umber

Leaf Green Dark
Leaf Green Medium
Leaf Green Light
Yellow Ochre

Burnt Sienna
Burnt Umber

1 Using a basecoat brush, prime the chest with white primer. Let the paint dry. Sand the surface and use a tack cloth to remove any sanding dust. Apply several coats of White semigloss latex, allowing the paint to dry between coats.

When the surface is dry, transfer the pattern using graphite paper and a stylus. Use repositionable tape to mask off the bands in the design and rub the tape edges down well. Use a palette knife to thin Pine Green semigloss latex with water. Apply this color to the taped-off bands using a glaze brush. Let the paint dry and carefully remove the tape.

To flyspeck the background, load a toothbrush with the thinned green and drag your thumb over the bristles, flicking paint onto the surface.

2 Using the palette knife, thin Yellow Ochre with water to a flowing consistency. Load the no. 2 script liner brush with the thinned paint and roll the brush on the palette to form a point. Stroke on vines around the green bands, creating an intertwining effect by painting some of the vines on top of the bands and letting others disappear behind them.

3 Load the script liner brush with thinned Burnt Sienna and stroke accents over the Yellow Ochre vines. Repeat with thinned Burnt Umber. To create dark leaves, load a no. 4 round brush with thinned Leaf Green Dark. Touch the brush to the surface, apply pressure, then lift the brush as you stroke upward to form the tip of the leaf.

4 Load the no. 4 round brush with thinned Leaf Green Medium and stroke on additional leaf shapes. Be sure to make a variety of leaf sizes by varying the amount of pressure you apply on the brush. Load the liner brush with thinned Leaf Green Dark and paint stems that connect the leaves to the vines.

5 Load a no. 4 flat shader brush with a thinned mixture of Alizarin Crimson and Burnt Umber paint. Stroke on berries by twisting the brush to form a loose circle. Scatter berries throughout the design. For the finishing touches, load the round brush with thinned Leaf Green Light and paint small, fine leaves.

6 Antique the entire chest by using a glaze brush to apply a thin mixture of Burnt Sienna and Burnt Umber. Immediately wipe off the desired amount of glaze with a cotton rag. Soften the effect by dusting the surface with the blending softener brush and the mop brush.

Monochromatic Painting: Daisies

Detail from daisies, leaves and cornflowers chest.

*T*his writing chest was decorated using a monochromatic (single color) palette. The daisies, leaves and cornflowers were painted in a range of blues, from light to dark. You can substitute other monochromatic palettes to create this design, such as yellows, creams, off-whites and greens. Just be sure to use a range of distinct values. A light strie finish provides a perfect background. 🐚

MONOCHROMATIC PAINTING: DAISIES

TOOLS AND MATERIALS

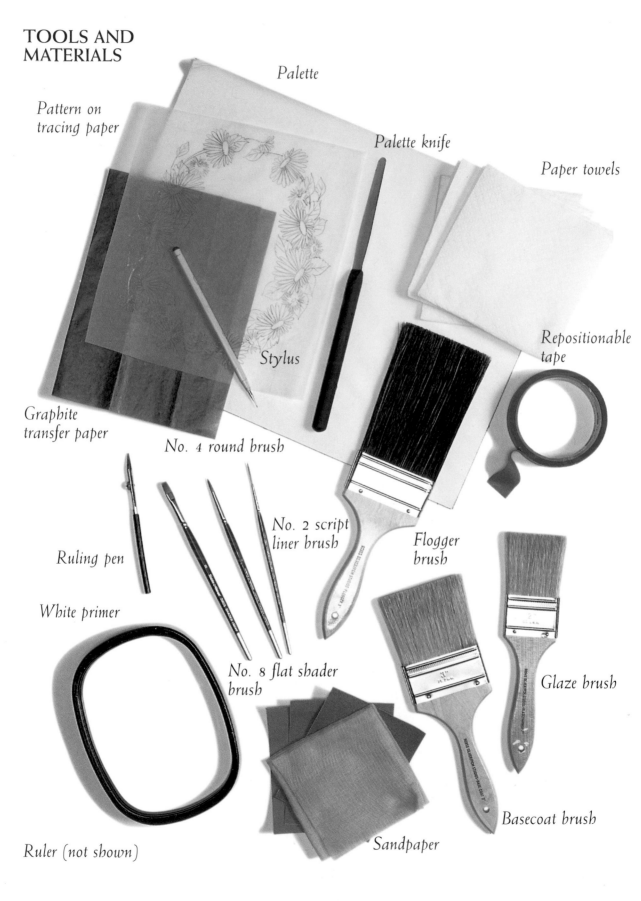

Palette

Pattern on tracing paper

Palette knife

Paper towels

Stylus

Repositionable tape

Graphite transfer paper

No. 4 round brush

No. 2 script liner brush

Flogger brush

Ruling pen

White primer

No. 8 flat shader brush

Glaze brush

Sandpaper

Basecoat brush

Ruler (not shown)

COLOR CHIPS—LATEX PAINT, WATER-BASED GLAZE, ARTIST'S ACRYLICS

White semigloss latex
Washed Denim glaze
Ultramarine Blue plus Mars Black

Light blue mix (White plus Ultramarine Blue
plus Mars Black)
Medium blue mix (White plus Ultramarine
Blue plus Mars Black)
Dark blue mix (White plus Ultramarine Blue
plus Mars Black)

1 Using a basecoat brush, prime the chest with white primer. Let the paint dry. Sand the surface lightly with a fine sandpaper and use a tack cloth to remove the sanding dust.

Use the basecoat brush to apply several coats of White semigloss latex, allowing the paint to dry between coats. Use a glaze brush to apply a Washed Denim glaze. Stroke through the wet glaze with a flogger brush to create a strie finish. Let the glaze dry.

Use a palette knife to thin White semigloss latex with water. Soften the blue into the background by applying the thinned White with the glaze brush and stroking through with the flogger brush.

MONOCHROMATIC PAINTING: DAISIES

2 Once the surface is dry, transfer the design using graphite paper and a stylus. Create three distinct values of blue—dark, medium and light—by mixing White, Ultramarine Blue and Mars Black in varying amounts.

To paint the leaves, double load a no. 8 flat shader brush with medium blue and dark blue. (For instructions on double loading your brush, turn to page 11.) Start at the base of the leaf and stroke the color on toward the edges. Wipe the brush lightly on a paper towel and use the dirty brush (a brush that still holds traces of color) to stroke light blue from the leaf's outside edges towards the center.

3 Using the palette knife, thin dark blue with water to a flowing consistency. Thin white, as well. Load a no. 4 round brush with the thinned blue. To paint the color-tinted daisies, stroke no more than three petals at a time with the blue—then immediately wipe your brush on a paper towel, load the dirty brush with the thinned white, and stroke over the blue.

4 To paint the cornflowers, load the no. 4 round brush with dark blue and stroke out from the center, creating a very ragged outside perimeter. Next, load the brush with medium blue and again stroke out from the center—only this time do not bring the color out as far. Finally, load your brush with light blue and add the light flower petals by painting a smaller, ragged starburst.

5 Now for the final touches. Load the round brush with a mixture of Ultramarine Blue and Mars Black and add dark, starburst centers to the cornflowers. Load a no. 2 script liner brush with thinned light blue and add veins to the leaves. Place all three values of blue on the daisy centers— dark blue on the left, medium blue in the middle and light blue on the right—and stroke blend the colors using the no. 8 flat shader brush. Add pollen dots loosely around the daisy centers using all three values of blue and pure white. Use a ruling pen to add a fine, dark blue trim.

VERDIGRIS FINISH: CHECKS

Detail from verdigris checked chest.

*P*atina finishes that suggest age and wear are among today's most popular decorating effects. They can bring an inviting, tactile quality to any project. The checks that form the pattern on this chest were created with a true verdigris finish. Actual copper was oxidized to achieve the chalky green patina that typically occurs when copper surfaces are exposed to rain, salt water and other elements. ৯

TOOLS AND MATERIALS

Kitchen sponge

Oxidizing chemicals—
Patina Green

Copper sheeting

Copper paint—
Copper Topper

No. 16 flat
shader brush

Spray mister
bottle

White craft glue

Sea sponge

Ruler

Permanent
marker—
fine-point black

Craft knife

Basecoat brush

White primer

Sandpaper

COLOR CHIP—LATEX PAINT

Black semigloss latex

1 Use a basecoat brush to prime the chest with white primer. Let the paint dry. Sand the surface and use a tack cloth to remove any sanding dust. Using the basecoat brush, apply several coats of Black semigloss latex until you achieve an opaque coverage. Allow paint to dry between coats.

VERDIGRIS FINISH: CHECKS

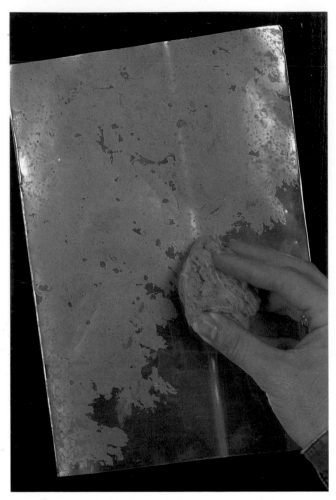

2 Using a craft knife with a ruler as a cutting edge, cut the copper sheeting into manageable sizes. Cut a panel for each side of the chest to ensure that you'll have plenty of extra copper to work with. Use the natural sea sponge to coat one side of each panel with Copper Topper—a substance that contains real copper particles. This will yield a more dramatic verdigris than oxidizing the copper sheeting directly.

3 While the sponged-on Copper Topper is still wet, fill a spray mister bottle with oxidizing chemicals (Patina Green) and mist the surface. As the chemicals react with the copper, a variety of green tones will form. Let the surface dry completely before proceeding.

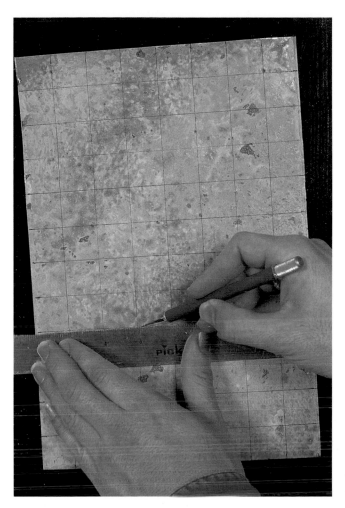

4 Use the ruler and a black fine-line permanent marker to measure off the desired check size. (The project shown uses 1-inch [2.5cm] squares.) Using the craft knife with a sharp blade, cut the copper first into strips, and then into individual squares.

5 Use a no. 16 flat shader brush to apply a thin layer of white craft glue on the back of each verdigris check. Mark the center of the top of the chest and place the first check there. Working outward from this starting point, place the checks on freehand, lining them up as evenly as possible. Don't worry if some pieces are slightly out of alignment. When you reach the outside edge, you'll need to cut the checks to fit.

Clean up the excess glue around the checks with a damp kitchen sponge. Let the checks dry.

FOLK ART PAINTING: LANDSCAPE

Detail from folk art landscape chest.

A landscape painting is an ideal way to decorate a chest. The scene can easily be designed to wrap around the sides and top of a chest, creating a sensational finished effect. For this chest, a casual painting approach was used to evoke a folk art look, but if you prefer, you can paint a more realistic and detailed landscape. This chest has been antiqued to give it an aged look and muted colors. For a different look, leave the colors of your landscape in full chroma intensity. ✺

TOOLS AND MATERIALS

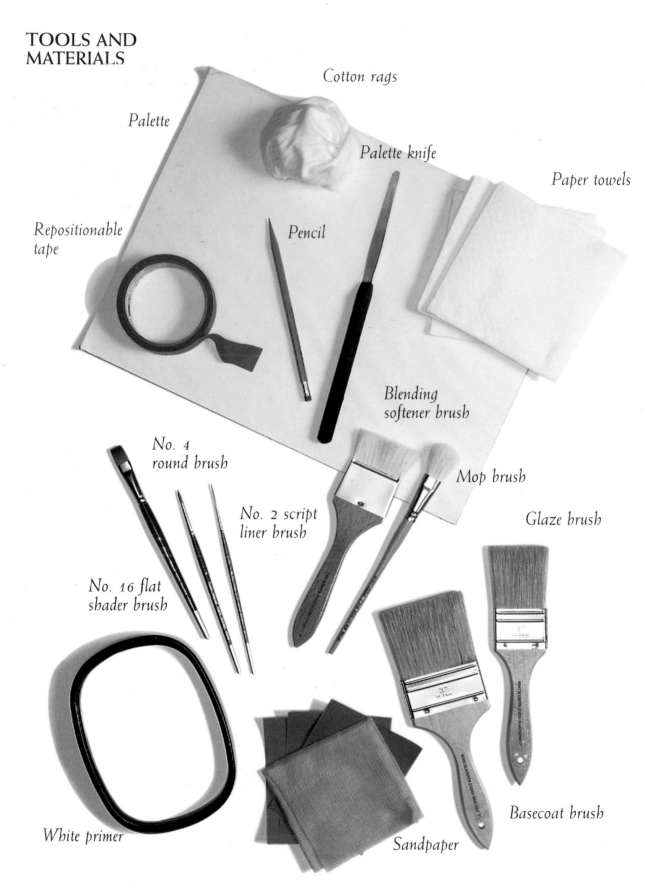

Cotton rags

Palette

Palette knife

Paper towels

Repositionable tape

Pencil

Blending softener brush

No. 4 round brush

Mop brush

No. 2 script liner brush

Glaze brush

No. 16 flat shader brush

White primer

Sandpaper

Basecoat brush

COLOR CHIPS—ARTIST'S ACRYLICS

Titanium White
Light blue mix (Titanium White plus
*   Ultramarine Blue plus Black)*
Medium blue mix (Titanium White plus
*   Ultramarine Blue plus Black)*
Dark blue mix (Ultramarine Blue plus
*   Black)*

Phthalo Green plus Yellow Ochre
Phthalo Green
Phthalo Green plus Black
Yellow Ochre

Black
Metallic Gold

1 Use a basecoat brush to prime the chest with white primer. Let the paint dry. Sand the surface with fine sandpaper and remove any sanding dust with a tack cloth. Apply several coats of Titanium White acrylic, allowing the paint to dry between coats.

Because of its simplistic nature, you can freehand paint this landscape. Just begin by using a pencil to sketch the horizon line of the rolling hills across the chest.

Create a medium value blue by mixing Titanium White, Ultramarine Blue and Black. Using a no. 16 flat shader brush, apply this mixture to the sky in loose, crisscross strokes to create a folk art look. Apply several coats, allowing the paint to dry between coats, until an opaque coverage is achieved.

2 Base the hills using a mixture of Phthalo Green and Yellow Ochre, applying several coats until an opaque coverage is achieved. Allow the paint to dry between coats.

Using a palette knife, thin Titanium White with water to a flowing consistency and side load the flat shader brush. (For instructions on side loading, turn to page 11.) To create the cloud shapes, stroke and layer upside-down U-shapes.

3 Create a light blue mixture of Titanium White, Ultramarine Blue and Black. Side load the flat shader brush with this blue and—using the same upside-down U-shapes—create smaller, distant cloud shapes below the primary clouds.

For the rolling hills, side load the flat shader brush with a mixture of Phthalo Green and Black. Stroke this dark shading color along each of the horizon-line hills. Place small dashes of Dark Blue mix on the background hills. Add the forward hills by loading the flat shader brush with Phthalo Green and Yellow Ochre (brush mixed) and using the chisel edge to create arching, linear strokes.

4 With a no. 4 round brush, add small dabs of Yellow Ochre to create field weeds. To paint the trees and bushes, load the round brush with Phthalo Green and Black and stroke on loose, triangular shapes using a dappling motion.

5 While the paint on the trees is still wet, use the round brush to dapple in lighter green tones and some pure Yellow Ochre. Using green mixes and Yellow Ochre, create more interest in the rolling hills by stroking arching shapes with a no. 2 script liner brush.

6 To antique the landscape, use a glaze brush to apply a very thin glaze in a black or brown tone. Wipe off excess glaze with a cotton rag. Soften the effect by dusting the surface with the blending softener brush and the mop brush.

Tape off the top edge with repositionable tape. Trim the top edge with Black. Let the paint dry. Add a Metallic Gold stripe with a liner brush.

FOLK ART PAINTING: ROOSTER

Detail from folk art rooster chest.

his kitchen chest features a whimsical painted rooster within a brushstroke border. Although red and yellow are the dominant colors in this particular piece, a rooster's tail feathers come in a rainbow of color choices, so you can easily alter the palette to suit your own decorating scheme. The color you choose for antiquing or overglazing will also greatly affect the look of the finished chest.

TOOLS AND MATERIALS

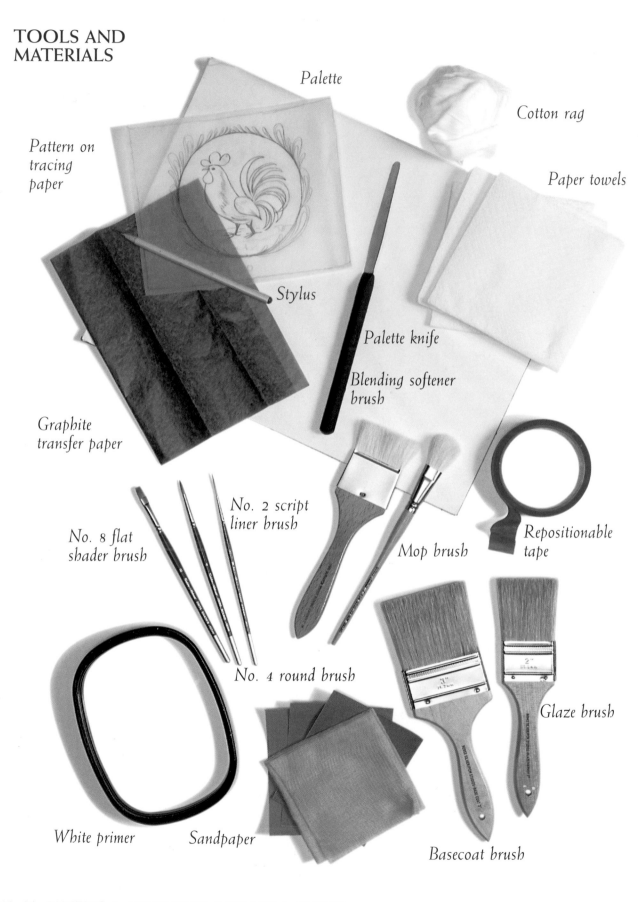

Palette

Cotton rag

Paper towels

Pattern on
tracing
paper

Stylus

Palette knife

Blending softener
brush

Graphite
transfer paper

No. 8 flat
shader brush

No. 2 script
liner brush

Mop brush

Repositionable
tape

No. 4 round brush

Glaze brush

White primer

Sandpaper

Basecoat brush

COLOR CHIPS—LATEX PAINT, ARTIST'S ACRYLICS

Ecru flat latex
Golden Ochre flat latex
Cadmium Yellow Light
Yellow Ochre

Bright Red
Alizarin Crimson
Burnt crimson mix (Alizarin Crimson plus
Burnt Umber)
Burnt Umber

Dark green mix (Black plus Cadmium
Yellow Light)
Black

1 Use a basecoat brush to prime the chest with white primer. Let the paint dry. Sand the surface and use a tack cloth to remove any sanding dust. Apply two coats of Golden Ochre flat latex, allowing the paint to dry between coats. Sand the dry surface with the grain of the wood to expose streaks of the white primer. If you like, you can sand down to expose some of the bare wood as well.

FOLK ART PAINTING: ROOSTER

2 Use graphite paper and a stylus to transfer the oval shape to your surface. Paint the oval in Ecru flat latex. Apply several coats, allowing the paint to dry between coats, until an opaque coverage is achieved. Let the last coat dry. Transfer the rooster and the brushstroke pattern.

Basecoat the brushstroke border with a dark green mixture of Black and Cadmium Yellow Light. Side load a no. 8 flat shader brush with the green mix and suggest the ground around the rooster's feet. (For instructions on side loading, turn to page 11.) Basecoat the rooster's comb, wattle and a few tail feathers in Bright Red; the beak, feet and a few tail feathers in Black; and the body and remaining tail feathers in Yellow Ochre.

3 Use a palette knife to thin Cadmium Yellow Light with water to a flowing consistency. Load a no. 4 round brush with this yellow and use the tip to highlight the rooster's comb, wattle, tail, wing, head and neck feathers. Load the round brush with a thinned mixture of Alizarin Crimson and Burnt Umber and establish shading on the red comb, wattle and tail feathers.

4 With Bright Red, overstroke the green border strokes—leaving a few of the smaller green strokes along the top and sides of the border as shown. Use the round brush loaded with Burnt Umber to develop dark shading on all the Yellow Ochre areas—lower to mid-body, wing feathers and tail feathers. Add small rock and pebbles around the rooster's feet with dabs of Burnt Umber and Black.

5 To add detail markings, load a no. 2 script liner brush with thinned Black. On the lower body, use short, choppy line strokes following the shape of the body. On the wing, use small U-strokes to suggest feathers. Use the handle end of your brush to add dots of thinned Bright Red to the border.

6 Antique the chest by applying thinned Burnt Umber with a glaze brush and wiping off the excess with a cotton rag. Soften the effect by dusting the surface with a blending softener brush and a mop brush.

PUNCHED WOOD: QUILTED DESIGN

Detail from punched-wood chest.

*T*his technique is normally executed on tin and other metal surfaces. Here, the technique has been adapted to give this wooden chest of drawers a quilted look. It is as if a needle and thread has punctured the surface with the crisscrossing pattern. The effect is quite simple to achieve; you'll just need a little patience and time to execute it successfully. The final overglazing step really emphasizes the punched-hole pattern. If you want to use a different design than the one shown here, quilt patterns can provide some great inspiration! ❧

TOOLS AND MATERIALS

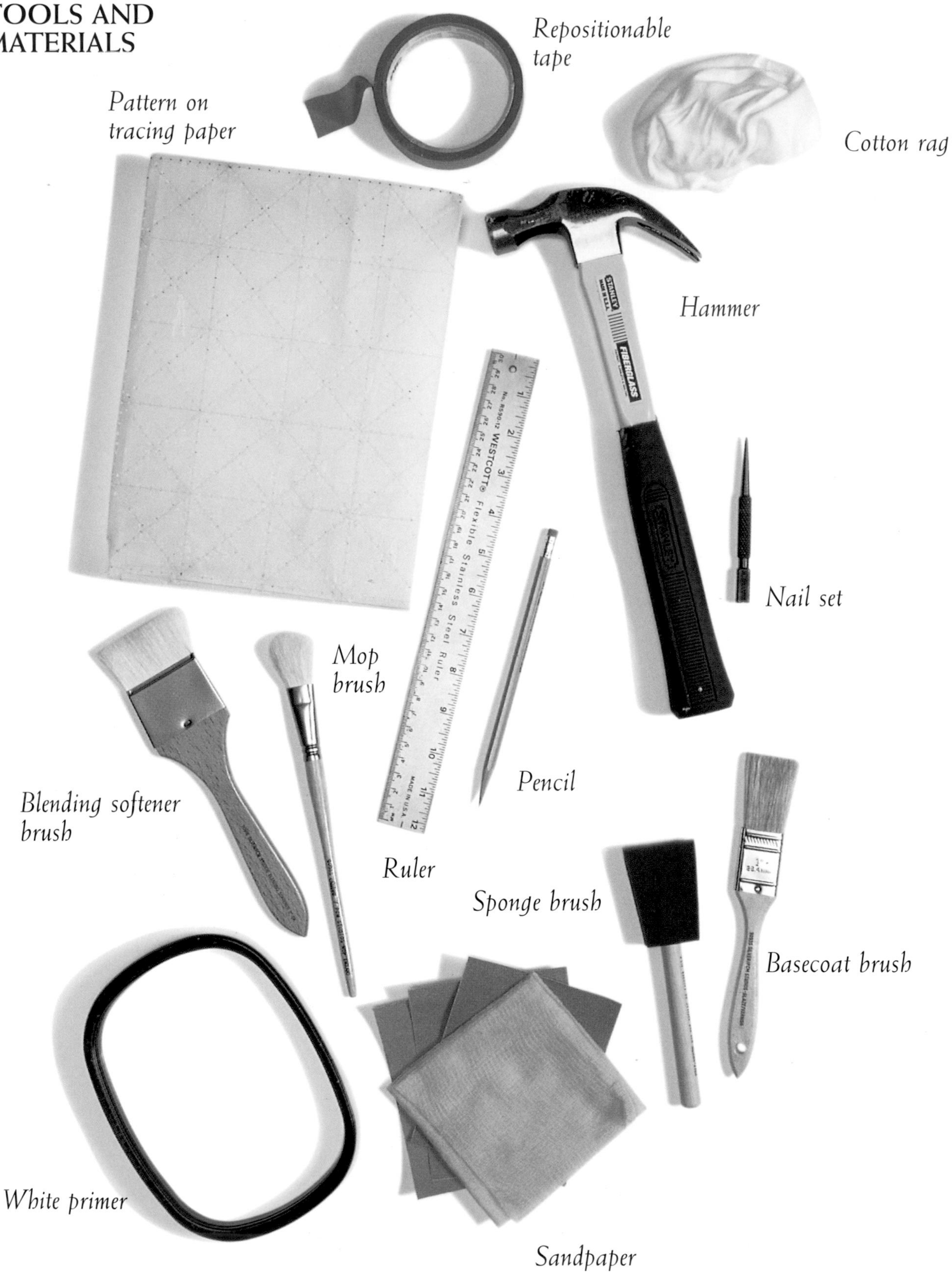

Repositionable tape

Pattern on tracing paper

Cotton rag

Hammer

Nail set

Mop brush

Pencil

Blending softener brush

Ruler

Sponge brush

Basecoat brush

White primer

Sandpaper

COLOR CHIPS—LATEX PAINT, WATER-BASED GLAZE

Bright Red semigloss latex
Black semigloss latex
Black glaze

1 Using a basecoat brush, prime the chest with white primer. Sand the surface with fine sandpaper and remove any sanding dust with a tack cloth. Using the basecoat brush, apply several coats of Bright Red semigloss latex—allowing the paint to dry between coats—to achieve an opaque coverage.

PUNCHED WOOD: QUILTED DESIGN

2 Using a pencil and a ruler, draw your punched pattern on tracing paper; instead of drawing solid lines, draw small dots about one quarter inch (6mm) apart. Use repositionable tape to secure the pattern in place on your surface.

"Punch" each dot using a hammer and a nail set. Try to strike each dot with equal force to create evenly sized holes.

3 As you "punch" your pattern, occasionally pull back the tracing paper to check the consistency of the hole sizes and to make sure you haven't missed any sections of the design. Before you resume marking holes, make sure that your pattern is properly and securely positioned. When you've completed one side of the chest, carefully remove the pattern and position it on the next side. Continue until all sides of the chest are punched.

4 Antiquing the chest accentuates the punched holes. Here, a Black glaze is used. Trim the top, bottom and around the drawers with Black semigloss latex. Let the paint dry. Apply the Black glaze with the sponge brush so you can squeeze excess glaze into the holes to darken them.

5 Use a cotton rag to wipe off the desired amount of Black glaze. Be sure to leave plenty of coloring in the punched holes. Soften the effect by dusting the surface with a blending softener brush and a mop brush.

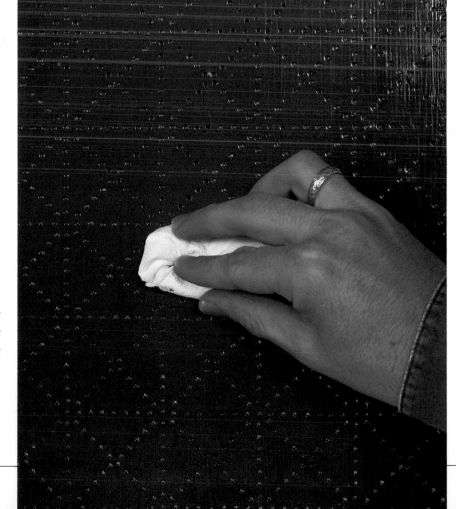

DECORATIVE PAINTING: LEAVES

Detail from decorative painted leaf chest.

Although most often thought of as background elements in a decorative design, leaves stand on their own beautifully when painted with detail and interest. While the leaves on this chest are painted in warm yellow tones for a summer mood, the palette can easily be altered for different effects—for example, blue tones for a spring feeling or brown tones for autumn. The background is created with a strie finish, providing a perfect linear backdrop to the flowing leaves. ❧

TOOLS AND MATERIALS

Pattern on tracing paper

Palette

Palette knife

Stylus

Paper towels

Graphite transfer paper

No. 8 flat shader brush

Repositionable tape

Flogger brush

Glaze brush

No. 2 script liner brush

White primer

Sandpaper

Turpentine (not shown)

Basecoat brush

COLOR CHIPS—LATEX PAINT, ARTIST'S OILS

Golden Ochre semigloss latex
Leaf Green
Ice Blue

Cadmium Yellow Medium
Burnt Sienna
Burnt Umber

1 Use a basecoat brush to prime the chest with white primer. Let the paint dry. Sand the surface and use a tack cloth to remove any sanding dust. Using a basecoat brush, apply several coats of Golden Ochre semigloss latex, allowing the paint to dry thoroughly between coats.

Thin the Leaf Green oil color with turpentine and apply it to the chest using a glaze brush. Stroke through the wet color with a flogger brush, creating a soft, dragged strie effect. Let the glaze dry.

2 Transfer the leaf pattern to your surface using graphite paper and a stylus.

To paint beautifully blended leaves, you should paint each individual leaf from start to finish before moving on to the next one. Begin by double loading a no. 8 flat shader brush with Leaf Green and Burnt Umber. (For instructions on double loading your brush, turn to page 11.) With the Burnt Umber on the outside edge, stroke a V-shape along the base of the leaf. With the Burnt Umber along the left side of the center vein, stroke along the center vein.

3 Load the flat shader brush with Leaf Green. Fill in the outside edges of the leaf, starting on the leaf's edge and stroking in towards the center. Wipe the brush lightly on a paper towel. (There will still be traces of the previous color on the bristles—this is called a "dirty brush.") Load the dirty brush with Cadmium Yellow Medium and fill in the area on the right side of the center vein.

DECORATIVE PAINTING: LEAVES

4 Blend the leaf using the flat shader brush. With a different color on each half of the brush, use short strokes to break up any sharp definitions between values and create a smooth blend.

Next, begin to establish the vein sections on the right side of the leaf by loading the flat shader brush with Ice Blue and pat blending out from the center vein in short diagonal streaks. Wipe the brush on a paper towel, load it with a small amount of Burnt Umber and pat blend the vein sections on the left side of the leaf.

5 Using the "dirty" flat shader brush, create vein lines down the center of the leaf and on the sides between the pat blended sections. Stroke the chisel edge through the paint to lift some of the color, creating a sharp vein line. If you cannot control the chisel edge of the flat brush to make the veins, use a liner brush.

6 Place an accent of a little Burnt Sienna on the leaf's edge and gently blend into the existing color. You can also use Burnt Sienna to create ragged edges or holes in the leaf for a rough, natural appearance.

FOLK ART PAINTING: FRUITS

The fruit on this chest has been painted in a spontaneous fashion, capturing the feeling of an apple, pear, cantaloupe and grapes without the exactness of a realistic rendering. Dabs of color are placed to create an optical blending of tones without the actual finessing of the paint with the brush. The antiquing of the finished painting also aids in the visual blending process. Graceful brushstrokes and simple dots trim out the oval-shaped design. 🥀

Detail from folk art fruit chest.

TOOLS AND MATERIALS

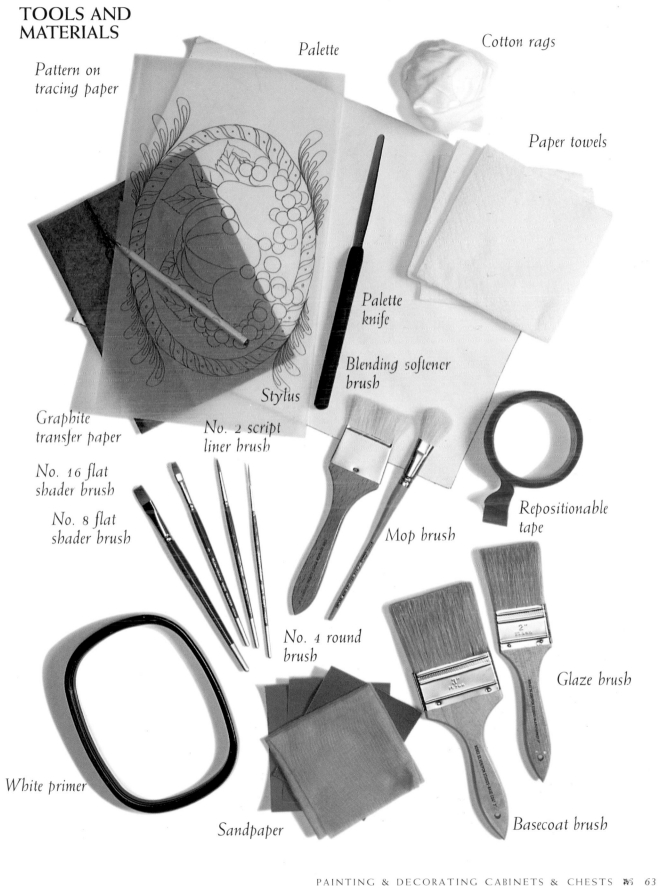

Pattern on tracing paper

Palette

Cotton rags

Paper towels

Palette knife

Blending softener brush

Stylus

Graphite transfer paper

No. 2 script liner brush

Repositionable tape

No. 16 flat shader brush

No. 8 flat shader brush

Mop brush

Glaze brush

No. 4 round brush

White primer

Sandpaper

Basecoat brush

COLOR CHIPS—LATEX PAINT, ARTIST'S ACRYLICS, WATER-BASED GLAZE

Red Oxide semigloss latex
Ecru semigloss latex
Titanium White
Cadmium Red Medium

Cadmium Yellow Light
Yellow Ochre
Leaf green mix (Cadmium Yellow Light plus
   Black)
Leaf green dark mix (Cadmium Yellow Light
   plus Ultramarine Blue plus Black)

Light blue mix (Titanium White plus
   Ultramarine Blue plus Black)
Medium blue mix (Titanium White plus
   Ultramarine Blue plus Black)
Ultramarine Blue
Dark blue mix (Ultramarine Blue plus
   Black)

Burnt Sienna
Mars Black
Brown glaze

1 Use the basecoat brush to prime the chest with white primer. Let the paint dry. Sand the surface and use a tack cloth to remove sanding dust. Use the basecoat brush to apply several coats of Red Oxide semigloss latex until an opaque coverage is achieved. Allow each coat to dry thoroughly before applying another.

2 Using graphite paper and a stylus, transfer the oval and band from the pattern to your surface. Paint the oval with Ecru semigloss latex and the band with Yellow Ochre.

Transfer the fruit design to your surface. Base the leaves and the cantaloupe with the leaf green dark mixture; the apple with Cadmium Red Medium; the pear with Yellow Ochre; and the grapes with the dark blue mixture. Apply several coats on all subjects until an opaque coverage is achieved.

3 Load a no. 4 round brush with the leaf green mix. Establish cantaloupe sections by dabbing color on the outside edge of each section of the cantaloupe, pouncing the brush with less and less pressure as you approach the darker crevasses.

Paint one leaf at a time with a fresh coat of the leaf green dark mixture and immediately overstroke with Cadmium Yellow Light, stroking from the leaf's edge towards the center vein. Let the paint dry. Side load a no. 8 flat shader brush with Black and darken the base of the leaves. (For instructions on side loading, see page 11.) Using a palette knife, thin Cadmium Yellow Light with water to a flowing consistency. Use a no. 2 script liner, loaded with thin yellow, to add veins.

4 Highlight the cantaloupe sections with dabs of Cadmium Yellow Light. Basecoat the medium-value grapes with the medium blue mixture using the no. 8 flat shader brush. Shade the apple with a no. 16 flat shader brush double loaded with Cadmium Red Medium and Burnt Sienna. (For instructions on double loading, turn to page 11.) Place color at the base of the apple where the grapes overlap it. Double load the no. 16 flat shader brush with Yellow Ochre and Burnt Sienna, and shade the pear along its base and right side.

5 Begin building a highlight area on the apple. (Brush mix these colors since you will need very small amounts.) Start by placing a circular shape towards the top left of the apple using Cadmium Red Medium plus Cadmium Yellow Light. Lighten this mixture with White and dab it on a smaller area. Finish the highlight with a pure dab of White.

Dab more Cadmium Yellow Light on the cantaloupe. Basecoat the light-value grapes with the light blue mix. To shade the grapes, side load the no. 8 flat shader brush, using dark blue mix for the medium-value grapes and the medium blue mix for the light grapes. Stroke along the right side of the grape, slightly inside the edge.

6 Build up the highlight on the pear by dabbing in circular shapes, decreasing in size, of Cadmium Yellow Light plus Yellow Ochre, then pure Cadmium Yellow Light, and finally pure White. Create markings on the pear with random dabs and dots of Burnt Sienna.

Dab pure White highlights on the cantaloupe. To highlight the forward grapes, dab light blue mix plus White on the upper left, finishing with a dot of White. To define the shapes of the grapes, outline them with thin light blue mix on a liner brush. For an accent color, add a stroke of Cadmium Red Medium. Paint the brushstroke border with Black, Yellow Ochre, Burnt Umber and White.

7 Antique the chest with a brown glaze, such as thinned Burnt Sienna or Burnt Umber. Use a glaze brush to apply the glaze and wipe off the desired amount with a cotton rag. Soften the effect by dusting the surface with a blending softener brush and a mop brush.

FROTTAGE: FLEUR-DE-LIS

Detail from frottage and fleur-de-lis chest.

$\mathcal{F}$rottage is a technique for creating visual texture by rubbing paper or fabric into wet paint. The fleur-de-lis is a stylized, three-petal iris used as an emblem of the kings of France. Combined on this chest in black, dark green and metallic gold, the two French-inspired motifs produce dramatic, high-style results.

TOOLS AND MATERIALS

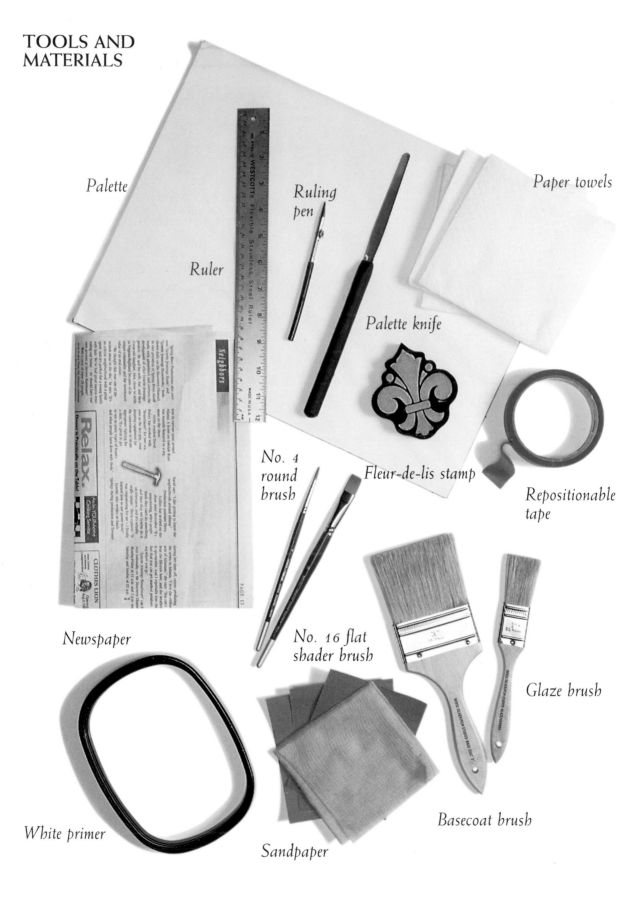

Palette

Ruler

Ruling pen

Palette knife

Paper towels

Fleur-de-lis stamp

Repositionable tape

No. 4 round brush

Newspaper

No. 16 flat shader brush

Glaze brush

Basecoat brush

White primer

Sandpaper

COLOR CHIPS—LATEX PAINT, WATER-BASED GLAZE, ARTIST'S ACRYLIC

Pine Green semigloss
latex
Black glaze
Metallic Gold

1 Using a basecoat brush, prime the chest with white primer and let the paint dry. Sand the surface with fine sandpaper and use a tack cloth to remove any sanding dust. Using the basecoat brush, base the chest with Pine Green semigloss latex. Apply several coats—allowing the paint to dry thoroughly between coats—until an opaque coverage is achieved. Allow the paint to thoroughly dry and cure before proceeding.

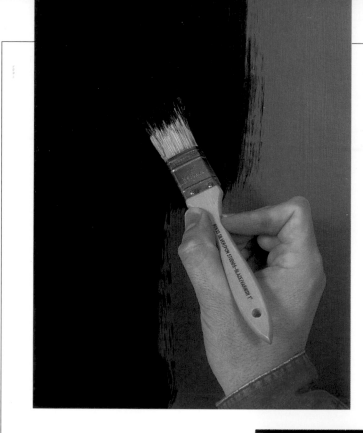

2 Use a glaze brush to apply Black glaze on one section of the chest at a time. You should complete steps 3 and 4 in this section before moving on to the next section. If your chest is small enough (no side larger than two feet square), you can glaze one side at a time. For larger chests, simply brush on the glaze in ragged patches no larger than two feet (61cm) square. The random frottage pattern will conceal where one section stops and the next begins.

3 Get a sheet of newspaper that is larger than the freshly glazed area. Crumple the newspaper, then smooth it out on a flat, dry surface. Next, starting from the edge of the glazed section, carefully lay the newspaper over the wet glaze.

4 Rub the newspaper with your hands, applying light, steady pressure. This will imprint the slightly wrinkled paper pattern into the wet glaze, absorbing some of the excess glaze in the process. After you have rubbed the entire surface, slowly lift off the newspaper. If the pattern on the chest is too dark, repeat this step using fresh pieces of wrinkled paper. Let the frottage pattern dry thoroughly.

5 Using the no. 16 flat shader brush, stroke an even coating of Metallic Gold paint on the fleur-de-lis stamp. Determine the center of your chest and firmly place the stamp there. Carefully lift up the stamp to prevent smearing. On large surfaces, you can stamp the design on newspaper first and then tape into position to evaluate the overall look before stamping the surface. Use a palette knife to thin Metallic Gold with water and load the paint into the pen with a round brush. Add ruling pen lines to trim out the chest.

The heart in the center of the chest lid reads "Chris & Richard Williams / October 17, 1987".

FOLK ART PAINTING: PEASANT COUPLE

Detail from folk art peasant couple chest.

*T*he style of this peasant couple painting mimics a New England artist named Peter Hunt. From the 1920s through the 1950s, Hunt painted with a vibrant, colorful palette and whimsical, folk art approach. His paintings were traditionally completed on a white background and then antiqued. To give this chest an aged look, a crackle finish was applied and then antiqued. The design could be easily adapted for a child's bedroom or nursery using pastel colors on a solid background. ❧

TOOLS AND MATERIALS

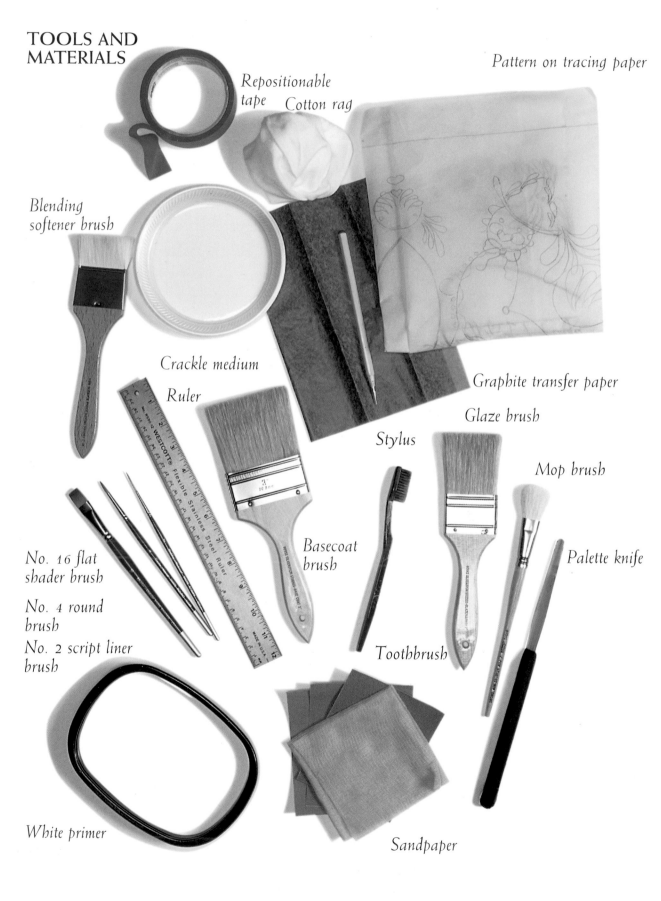

Repositionable tape

Cotton rag

Pattern on tracing paper

Blending softener brush

Crackle medium

Ruler

Graphite transfer paper

Glaze brush

Stylus

Mop brush

No. 16 flat shader brush

No. 4 round brush

No. 2 script liner brush

Basecoat brush

Palette knife

Toothbrush

White primer

Sandpaper

COLOR CHIPS—LATEX PAINT, ARTIST'S ACRYLICS

Ecru semigloss latex
Titanium White
Cadmium Red Light
Cadmium Red Medium

Light pink mix (Titanium White plus
*   Cadmium Red Medium)*
Medium pink mix (Titanium White plus
*   Cadmium Red Medium)*
Dark pink mix (Titanium White plus
*   Cadmium Red Medium)*
Burnt Umber

Leaf Green
Leaf Green Dark
Light blue mix (Ultramarine Blue plus
*   White)*
Ultramarine Blue

Black

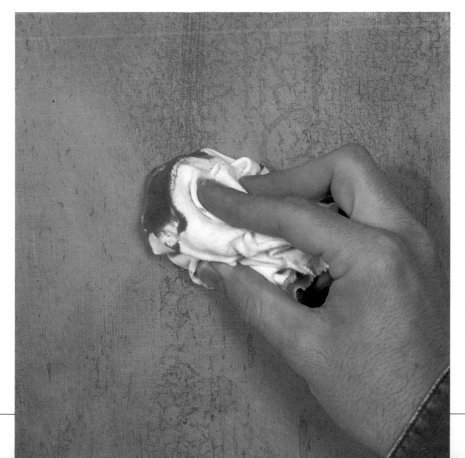

1 Using a basecoat brush, prime the chest with white primer. Let the paint dry. Sand the chest with fine sandpaper and remove the sanding dust with a tack cloth. Use the basecoat brush to base the chest in several coats of Ecru semigloss latex—allowing the paint to dry between coats—until an opaque coverage is achieved.

When the paint is thoroughly dry, follow the manufacturer's directions to apply the crackle medium. Let the medium dry.

Using a palette knife, thin Burnt Umber to a flowing consistency and apply with a glaze brush. Wipe off excess glaze with a cotton rag, letting the glaze collect in the cracks.

2 Transfer the design using graphite paper and a stylus. Using a basecoat brush, basecoat the design using the following colors: Cadmium Red Medium for the heart; Cadmium Red Light for the ball flowers; Black for the man's hat, bow tie and feet; the light blue mix for the man's shirt; White for his socks; the dark pink mix for the lady's hat and skirt; the medium pink mix for her blouse; and the light pink mix for the couple's faces and hands.

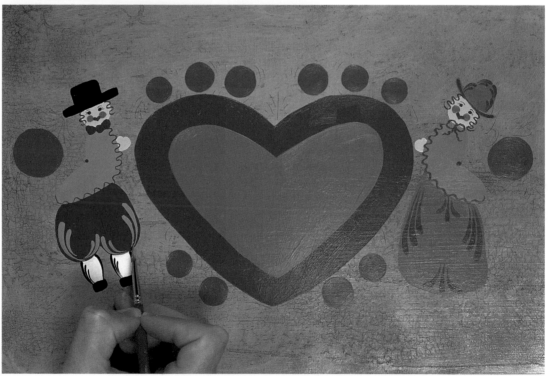

3 Load a no. 16 flat shader brush with the dark pink mix and paint another heart shape within the larger heart. On the couple's faces, paint dark pink mix circles for cheeks; Black eyes, eyebrows and hair; and heart-shaped mouths using Cadmium Red Medium. Using a no. 4 round brush and a no. 2 script liner brush, add brushstrokes and details on the lady's clothing with thin Cadmium Red Medium. Load the liner brush with thin Black and add brushstrokes and details to the man's socks and shirt. Add brushstrokes on his pants with the light blue mix.

4 Using the no. 4 round brush and thin light pink mix, add a series of four comma strokes on the top of each ball flower. Add a dot of light pink mix on each ball flower. Load the brush with thin Leaf Green Dark and place in the dark brushstroke leaves.

5 Use the no. 4 round brush and thin Leaf Green to add the remaining brushstroke leaves. If you wish, you can personalize the painting by thinning black or dark green paint to an ink-like consistency and stroking on important names and dates with the script liner brush.

6 Antique the painting with a glaze using an earth-tone color such as Burnt Umber. Brush on the color with a glaze brush and wipe off excess glaze with a cotton rag. Dust a blending softener brush and a mop brush over the surface to soften the effect, leaving recessed areas and corners darker for contrast. Flyspeck the surface with glaze using a toothbrush.

DECORATIVE PAINTING: ROSES

Roses are a perennial favorite among decorative painters. Here, pink roses are painted among lilacs and leaves, turning a simple chest into one worthy of storing wedding memorabilia and other special keepsakes. Learning how to paint beautiful stroke roses takes time and practice. But once you learn how to load your brush and you master the individual strokes, painted roses will be forever blooming from your brush! ❧

Detail from decorative roses chest.

TOOLS AND MATERIALS

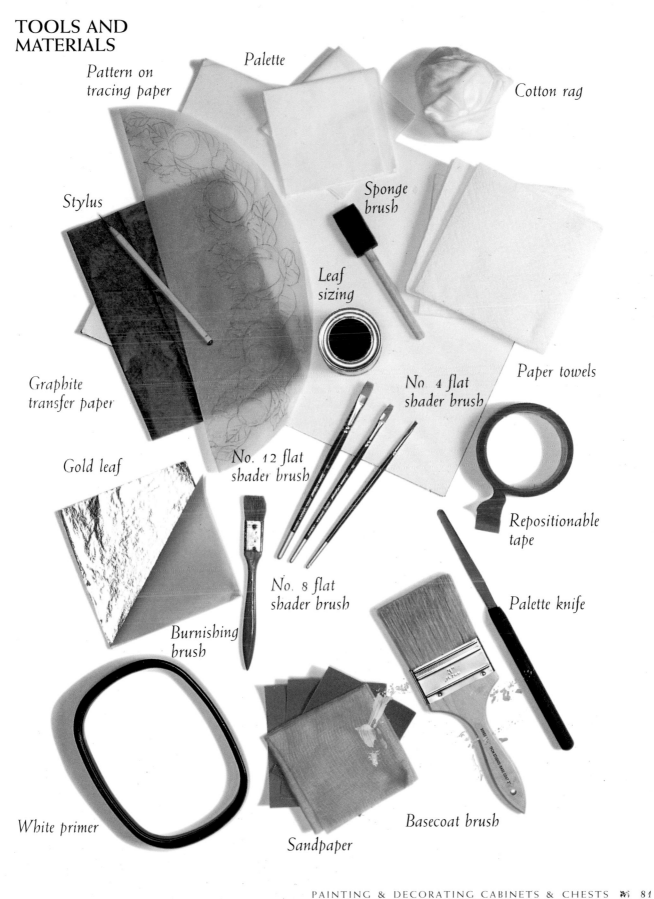

Pattern on
tracing paper

Palette

Cotton rag

Stylus

Sponge
brush

Leaf
sizing

Graphite
transfer paper

No. 4 flat
shader brush

Paper towels

Gold leaf

No. 12 flat
shader brush

Repositionable
tape

No. 8 flat
shader brush

Palette knife

Burnishing
brush

White primer

Sandpaper

Basecoat brush

COLOR CHIPS—LATEX PAINT, ARTIST'S OILS

Ecru semigloss latex
Titanium White
Ice Blue
Leaf Green

Light pink mix (Titanium White plus
*   Alizarin Crimson plus Burnt Umber)*
Medium pink mix (Titanium White plus
*   Alizarin Crimson plus Burnt Umber)*
Dark pink mix (Titanium White plus
*   Alizarin Crimson plus Burnt Umber)*
Burnt crimson mix (Alizarin Crimson plus
*   Burnt Umber)*

Burnt Sienna
Burnt Umber
Prussian Blue plus Burnt Umber
Prussian Blue

1 Use the basecoat brush to prime the chest with white primer. Let the paint dry. Sand the surface and use a tack cloth to remove the sanding dust. Basecoat the chest with Ecru semigloss latex. Apply several coats, allowing to dry between coats, until an opaque coverage is achieved. When the paint is thoroughly dry, transfer the pattern to your surface using graphite paper and a stylus.

To create a shaded background, start by double loading a no. 12 flat shader brush with Leaf Green on one side and a mix of Prussian Blue and Burnt Umber on the other side. (For instructions on double loading, turn to page 11.) With the dark color against the edge of the design, stroke a small section at a time. Then, using your fingertips and a facial tissue, pounce the color to create a soft blend outward from the design's edge.

2 To paint the leaves, double load a no. 8 flat shader brush with Leaf Green on one side and a mix of Prussian Blue and Burnt Umber on the other. Place dark color at the base of the leaf and up the left side of the vein. Fill in the rest of the leaf with Leaf Green. Load the brush with Ice Blue and pat blend side vein sections. (For instructions on pat blending, turn to page 11.) Highlight some leaf edges with strokes of Ice Blue pulled inward. Scribe on vein lines by stroking the chisel edge of the dirty flat shader brush through the paint. (A "dirty" brush is one that has been wiped on a paper towel but still holds traces of color.) Stroke accents onto the leaves using colors from the roses and lilacs as well as a little Burnt Sienna.

3 To paint the lilacs, use the no. 8 flat shader brush to loosely dab on patches of Prussian Blue and a mix of Alizarin Crimson and Burnt Umber. Brush mix these color patches on the surface. This casual placement will create a variety of colors, from blue to purple to pink. Create individual flower petals by overstroking the color patches using a no. 4 flat shader brush loaded with thin, creamy Titanium White. To create variations of color in the lilac clump, stroke the brush several times into the wet color patches before loading with fresh white.

4 To create roses with beautiful color variations, double load the no. 12 flat shader brush—medium pink mix or dark pink mix on one side and a mix of Alizarin Crimson and Burnt Umber on the other side. Following the step-by-step photos on page 85, first stroke on the back scalloped petals and then the front bowl petals.

5 Continue to develop the roses as illustrated in the step-by-step photos: fill in the throat of the rose and place the side and lower petals. Pick up a small amount of light pink mix on the lighter side of the dirty double-loaded brush. Lighten the center rose by restroking the front bowl petals, a few side petals and the small, filler petals in the throat of the rose.

To trim the edge of the chest with gold leaf, brush on gold leaf sizing with a sponge brush, allow the sizing to reach a tacky state, then carefully apply gold leaf sheets. Let this dry overnight. Burnish off the excess leaf pieces with a soft burnishing tool and a cotton rag.

CREATING A STROKE ROSE STEP-BY-STEP

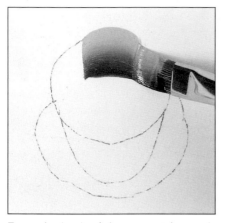

Form the back of the rose with a scalloped arc stroke.

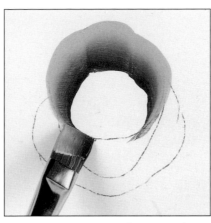

Paint two comma strokes on either side of the arc stroke.

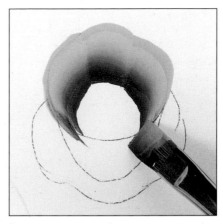

Repeat steps, stroking on a second layer of petals slightly lower.

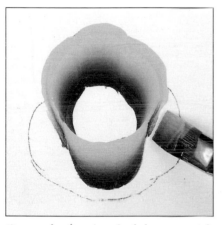

Create the first bowl of the rose with a U-stroke.

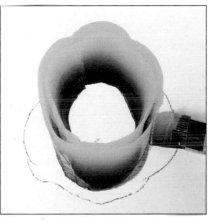

Drop a second bowl of the rose lower, stroking on another U-stroke.

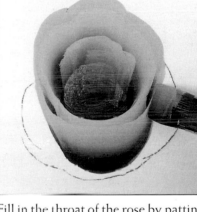

Fill in the throat of the rose by patting the brush upward. Restroke the bowl.

Develop side petals by stroking on sliced comma strokes.

Add lower level of side petals with smaller, slice-like comma strokes.

Add center lower petal by stroking on a "lazy" S-stroke.

Apple Cinnamon

Orange Pekoe

Lemon Zinger

English Tea Time

Chamomile

Breakfast Time

DIMENSIONAL STENCILING: TEACUPS

English Tea Time

Detail from dimensional stenciled chest.

*H*ave you ever seen a chest of drawers more ideal for housing all your favorite teas? The teacups were stenciled with dimensional paste. The texture created on the surface and the shadows cast by the "teacups" evoke a very inviting, tactile feeling. Here, a design of roses, buds and leaves decorates the teacups, but you can use any motif you like . . . even one that matches your own china or dinnerware pattern. ✄

DIMENSIONAL STENCILING: TEACUPS

TOOLS AND MATERIALS

Computer printout of tea titles

Pattern on tracing paper

Decoupage glue

English Tea Time
Earl Grey
Breakfast Time
Sleepy Time
Apple Cinnamon
Chamomile
Plantation Mint
Lemon Zinger
Orange Pekoe

Stylus

Kitchen sponge

Dimensional paste

Sponge brush

Brayer

No. 2 script liner brush

Ruler

Trowel

No. 4 flat shader brush

Dimensional stencil

Craft knife

Basecoat brush

Repositionable tape

Palette knife

Graphite transfer paper

Sandpaper

Palette (not shown)
White primer (not shown)

COLOR CHIPS—LATEX PAINT, ARTIST'S OILS

Cornflower Blue semigloss latex
Titanium White
Ice Blue
Cadmium Yellow Medium

Medium pink mix (Titanium White plus
  Alizarin Crimson plus Burnt Umber)
Leaf Green
Burnt crimson mix (Alizarin Crimson plus
  Burnt Umber)
Prussian Blue

Burnt Umber

1 Use the basecoat brush to prime your chest with white primer. Sand the surface and remove sanding dust with a tack cloth. Basecoat the surface with several coats of Cornflower blue semigloss latex.

Decide what type of tea you want to keep in each drawer. Type the names of these teas on a computer, specifying an attractive type style and an appropriate point size. Print out several copies (to allow for error). Using a ruler and a craft knife, cut apart the titles so that you have strips of paper—one label for each drawer.

Using a sponge brush, coat the back of the labels with decoupage glue and center the labels along the bottom edge of the drawer fronts. Use the brayer to smooth out the labels, and clean up excess glue with a sponge.

2 Center the dimensional stencil on the drawer front and secure it in place with repositionable tape. Use a palette knife to scoop dimensional paste out of the container and spread it in the stencil until the teacup design is completely filled. Scrape across the stencil with the plastic trowel to remove excess paste. It will probably take two or three swipes to even out the paste in the stencil.

3 It is very important to carefully and slowly remove the stencil from the surface. Careless or quick removal may cause the texture to deflate and the pattern to slide downward. If this happens, you have two options: Simply scrape off the paste and start over again; or use a damp brush to carefully remove paste outside the design lines, let the remaining dimension dry, and repeat step 2.

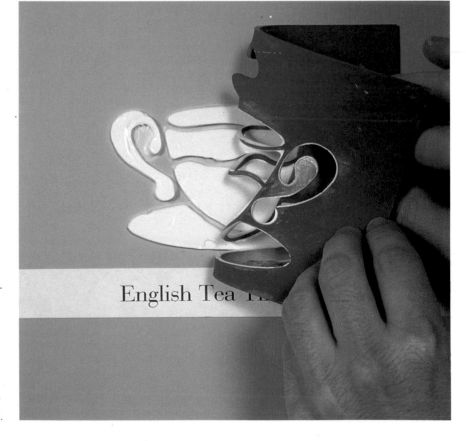

4 After the dimension has dried overnight, you can decorate as desired. Trace and transfer your desired pattern. In this sample, small roses and rosebuds are created using a no. 4 flat shader brush double loaded with medium pink mix and burnt crimson mix. (For step-by-step instructions on stroking a rose, turn to page 85.)

5 To add leaves, use the flat shader brush double loaded with Leaf Green and a mix of Prussian Blue and Burnt Umber. (For instructions on double loading, turn to page 11.) Stroke dark color at the base of the leaves and along the left side of the vein. Highlight the leaves with strokes of Cadmium Yellow Medium and Ice Blue pulled from the edges towards the center of the leaves. Using a no. 2 script liner brush, place small strokes and leaves around the rosebuds with Leaf Green and Ice Blue, each thinned with water.

DECORATIVE PAINTING: BAROQUE FLORALS

Detail from baroque floral chest

*B*aroque refers to the style of art and architecture developed in Europe from the 1500s to the 1700s. This style embraced elaborate, ornate scrolls and filigree in everything from art to furniture to buildings. On this chest of drawers, scrolls are painted in several tones and combined with roses, daisies and leaves for exciting results. The design flows across the entire front of the chest—curved drawers and all. ✑

TOOLS AND MATERIALS

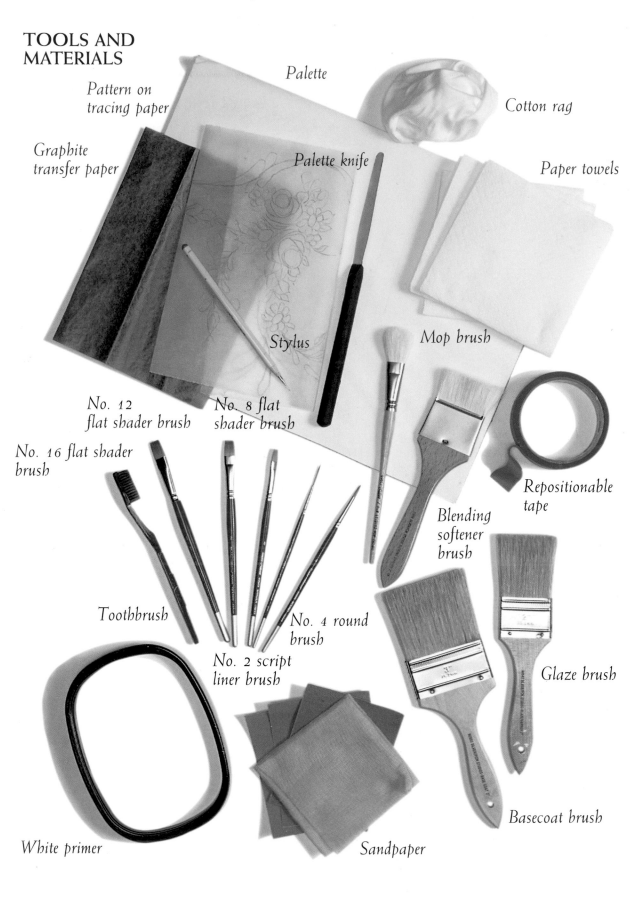

Pattern on tracing paper

Palette

Cotton rag

Graphite transfer paper

Palette knife

Paper towels

Stylus

Mop brush

No. 12 flat shader brush

No. 8 flat shader brush

No. 16 flat shader brush

Repositionable tape

Toothbrush

No. 4 round brush

Blending softener brush

No. 2 script liner brush

Glaze brush

White primer

Sandpaper

Basecoat brush

COLOR CHIPS—LATEX PAINT, ARTIST'S ACRYLICS

Ecru semigloss latex
Cadmium Yellow Light
Yellow Ochre

Light blue-green mix (Titanium White plus
*   Ultramarine Blue plus Phthalo Green)*
Ultramarine Blue
Phthalo Green

Burnt crimson mix (Alizarin Crimson plus
*   Burnt Umber)*
Burnt Sienna
Burnt Umber

1 Using a basecoat brush, prime the chest with white primer and let the paint dry. Sand the surface with fine sandpaper and remove any sanding dust with a tack cloth. Using the basecoat brush, apply several coats of Ecru semigloss latex until an opaque coverage is achieved. Allow each coat to dry thoroughly before applying the next coat.

2 Transfer the pattern to your surface using graphite paper and a stylus. Basecoat the border scrolls in Burnt Sienna; the roses in Cadmium Yellow Light or the burnt crimson mix; the daisies in either Ultramarine Blue, the burnt crimson mix or White; and the leaves in Phthalo Green.

3 Overstroke the border scrolls in Yellow Ochre. One at a time, recoat each leaf in Phthalo Green, then immediately overstroke it with a no. 8 flat shader brush loaded with the light blue-green mix. Pull the color on from the edge of the leaf towards the center. Next, use a palette knife to thin Ultramarine Blue with water. Load a no. 2 script liner brush with this color and stroke center veins on the leaves. Brighten some leaves by adding an additional light stroke of the light blue-green mix.

4 Apply a second coat of Yellow Ochre on the border scrolls.

Thin the Ultramarine Blue to use as the color tint for the blue and white daisies; thin a mix of Alizarin Crimson and Burnt Umber to use on the pink daisies. To paint the color-tinted daisy petals, follow this method: Using a no. 12 flat shader brush, stroke the thinned color on one petal at a time. Immediately wipe the brush lightly on a paper towel and load the "dirty" brush with White. Stroke blend the brush on the palette to soften the White into a lighter value of the color tint placed on the petal, and overstroke this brush-mixed color on the still-wet petal.

Paint the daisy centers in Cadmium Yellow Light and shade them with Burnt Sienna. Use a no. 4 round brush to add pollen dots of Burnt Sienna, Cadmium Yellow Light and White.

5 Brush mix the Ecru base paint with Cadmium Yellow Light and overstroke the border scrolls. Paint the roses with a double-loaded no. 16 flat shader brush— Burnt Sienna and Cadmium Yellow Light for yellow roses, burnt crimson mix and a mix of White and the burnt crimson mix for pink roses. Paint the stroke roses by following the step-by-step demonstration on page 85.

6 Antique the chest with brown tones. (Here, a thin mix of Burnt Umber and Burnt Sienna was used.) Use a glaze brush to apply the glaze, then wipe off the desired amount using a cotton rag. Soften the effect by dusting the surface with a blending softener brush and a mop brush. Flyspeck the chest by loading a toothbrush with the brown tones and dragging your thumb over the bristles.

MARQUETRY: WOOD STAINING

Detail from marquetry wood-stained chest.

Marquetry is the inlaying of wood or ivory to create a design on a surface. The same effect has been achieved on this chest by masking off sections and staining them different colors. A traditional tumbling block pattern was used here, but a variety of graphic designs, including quilt patterns, can be used as inspirations for your marquetry wood staining. A standard earth-tone palette was chosen to further the illusion of inlaid wood, but you could render the same design using a colorful palette. ❧

TOOLS AND MATERIALS

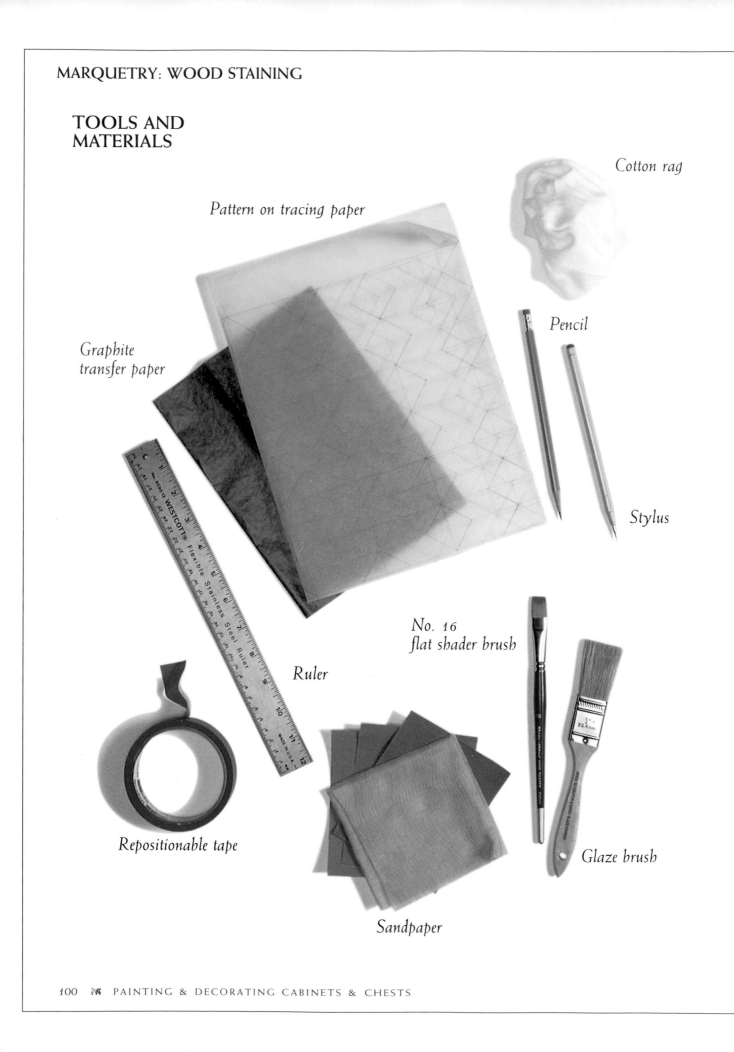

Cotton rag

Pattern on tracing paper

Graphite
transfer paper

Pencil

Stylus

Ruler

No. 16
flat shader brush

Repositionable tape

Sandpaper

Glaze brush

COLOR CHIPS—WATER-BASED GLAZES

Old Gold
Old Gold plus Indian
   Brown

Dark Brown
Black

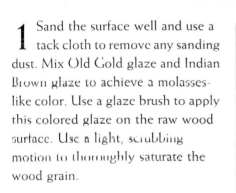

1 Sand the surface well and use a tack cloth to remove any sanding dust. Mix Old Gold glaze and Indian Brown glaze to achieve a molasses-like color. Use a glaze brush to apply this colored glaze on the raw wood surface. Use a light, scrubbing motion to thoroughly saturate the wood grain.

2 Use a cotton rag to remove excess glaze from the surface, revealing the wood grain. If you are working on a large surface, apply and wipe off the glaze in manageable sections. When you're finished, one section should blend smoothly into the next without any visible distinction. Let this background stain dry overnight.

3 Position the pattern and secure it in place using repositionable tape. Slip graphite paper under the pattern. Using a stylus and a ruler, carefully trace the pattern lines. Your pattern lines must be sharp and precise to successfully create the stained design.

4 Carefully mask off individual shapes using repositionable tape. Rub the edges down firmly to prevent the stain from bleeding. (If you are completing an involved pattern, such as this one with one section butting up against another, you'll need to mask off one shape at a time.) Using a no. 16 flat shader brush, place the Dark Brown glaze on alternating shapes. Allow to dry overnight.

5 Once the brown shapes are thoroughly dry, repeat step 4 to glaze the alternating shapes with Black glaze. (If you attempt to proceed before the Brown stain is completely dry, the tape will not stick and the Black glaze will bleed.)

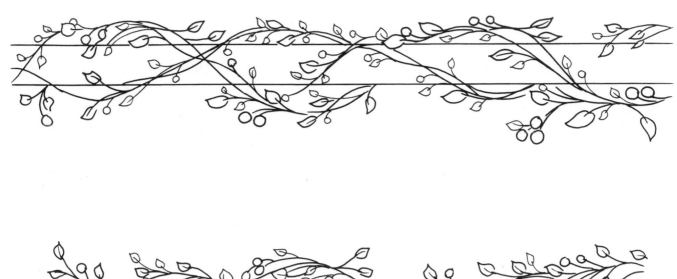

GLOSSARY

ACRYLIC POLYMER—a thermoplastic resin, with a synthetic substance or mixture, used as a binder with powdered pigments in the creation of artist's acrylic colors.

ANTIQUING—the application of a very thin, transparent coating over a surface to create the illusion of age and patina.

ARTIST'S ACRYLIC COLORS—paint that is a mixture of powdered pigments ground in thermoplastic, synthetic emulsions, which can be thinned and cleaned up with water.

ARTIST'S OIL COLORS—paint that is a mixture of powdered pigment ground in linseed oil. It must be thinned and cleaned up with mineral spirits or turpentine.

BASECOAT—the initial application of paint to a surface.

BODY—the consistency or thickness of paint.

BRAYER—a small "hand roller" tool used to apply pressure.

BURNISH—to polish or rub a surface with a hard tool to adhere paper or gold leaf to the surface and smooth areas.

CHISEL EDGE—the sharp edge on the bristle ends of a well-crafted flat brush.

COLOR VALUES—the degrees of lightness, darkness, saturation and brightness of a hue.

CRACKLED—random separations in a paint or varnish finish, making the object appear older than it really is; can result from product incompatibility, temperature or weather.

CRISSCROSS—a paint stroke direction that forms randomly crossed lines.

CURTAINING—the sagging or dripping of a layer of paint or varnish which has been placed over a previous coat that was not fully cured and dried.

DAPPLING—the creation of mottled or spotted markings on a surface through the application of small dabs of color, usually completed with thin consistency paint and the tip of a round brush.

DARK VALUE—the deeper color tones that can be created by mixing any color with black or its color complement.

DECOUPAGE—the French art form of cutting and pasting down images to form decorative treatments on a surface.

DIRTY BRUSH—a brush that has been loaded with color and used in the painting process, then—instead of being cleaned—is just wiped lightly on a paper towel so that traces of paint remain on its bristles.

DISTRESSING—the action of battering a surface through the use of abrasive tools such as sandpaper, hammers, nails, screws or chains; the goal is to imitate the wear and tear of an aged surface.

DOUBLE LOAD—to carry two colors on a brush at one time, side by side, with a smooth color gradation between them.

DRY-BRUSH BLENDING—to gradate and create a smooth color transition by stroking over a freshly painted surface with a dirty brush,

using no thinning medium or solvent.

EARTH TONES—colors that are made with natural pigments (like Yellow Ochre, which is made from refined clay).

FAUX—the French word which translates as false or fake; as it relates to painted finishes, a painted look which mimics marble, wood grain and other natural surfaces.

FLAT—a sheen or finish that is dull and porous.

FLYSPECKING—the painting technique that disperses small particles of thin paint over the surface with the use of a toothbrush.

FOLK ART PAINTING—a naive, primitive style of painting which is rendered in a loose, casual approach—often created by an individual who is without formal training and is self-taught.

FREEHAND—to create without the use of patterns or guidelines.

GLAZE—a transparent mixture of color plus a clear painting medium.

GLOSS—the highest level of a finish's sheen or shine qualities.

GRAY SCALE—a standardized, incremental chart of values from white to black (light to dark).

GRID—a framed structure of equally spaced parallel and perpendicular lines used to paint various tile or stripe patterns; also used to enlarge or reduce the size of designs by scaling them up or down proportionately.

HUE—the qualities of color; the intensity of color, as in a shade or tint.

INK-LIKE CONSISTENCY—paint thinned with painting medium,

painting glaze or solvent to the liquid state that matches drawing ink.

LATEX—paint made from powdered pigment ground with emulsion of rubber or plastic globules; can be cleaned with water.

LIFT OFF—the intentional or accidental removal of a base coat, paint finish or varnish.

LIGHT VALUE—the brighter color values on the gray scale; any color can become a lighter value through the addition of white.

MARBLEIZING—the act of reproducing a marble pattern through the use of paint applied with a brush and/or feathers on a surface.

MASKING—to protect an area by covering it with tape or other materials so that it won't receive paint when a nearby area is being painted.

MEDIUM—the type of paint used, such as acrylics or oils; or a liquid, such as water-based varnish, acrylic retarder or water, used to thin acrylic paints.

MEDIUM VALUE—a color tone in the middle of the value range between light and dark.

MONOCHROMATIC—pertaining to one color tone.

MULTITONE—the development of a variety of values of one color or many colors on a surface.

OPAQUE—paint coverage thick enough that light cannot pass through it.

OPEN TIME—the period in which paints, painting mediums or varnishes will remain workable before they begin to set up and dry.

PAINT RUNS—usually undesirable drips of paint or varnish that move down a vertical surface.

PATINA—the characteristic marks and signs of age that develop on a surface; the corrosion that occurs as metals oxidize.

PATTERN—a guideline to follow when creating.

PRIMER—an opaque, paint-like basecoat application that seals the surface and readies it for decorative treatment; a stain-blocking sealer that prevents bottom coats from penetrating through.

RETARDER—agents that suspend and slow down the quick drying time of some water-based products such as acrylics.

RULING—the painted trim work of fine lines created through the application of thin paint with a ruling pen.

SAGGING—the lifting and dropping of a coat of paint due to improper surface preparation.

SATIN—a surface with a slight amount of sheen or shine.

SCRIPT—handwriting with cursive characters as opposed to printing.

SEMIGLOSS—a sheen level between satin and gloss.

SETUP TIME—the period it takes for paint, painting glazes or varnishes to begin to dry and become tacky.

SIDE LOAD—to carry color on one side of the brush only with painting medium or solvent on the other; to create a blended transition on the brush from opaque color to transparent color to no color.

SIZING—an adhesive used in the gilding process, brushed on to attach metal leaf to a surface.

SOLVENT—the agent that cleans and thins such materials as paint, varnishes and painting mediums. A paint's solvent can be used as a painting medium; the solvent for acrylic is water, the solvent for oils is turpentine.

SPONGING—the application of paint using a sponge to create a textural pattern on a surface.

STAMPING—the process of imprinting a surface with a design or pattern using a rubber or foam cutout.

STENCIL—a sheet of Mylar, acetate or heavy card stock with a design cut into it.

STENCILING—the application of design work by brushing or spraying paint through a cut design opening.

STIPPLING—the action of pouncing a brush up and down in an upright manner to deposit a fine dot like pattern that can be built anywhere from a light to dense application of paint or glaze on a surface.

STRIE—the painted finish technique that uses a flogger brush to create irregular linear streaks in a wet paint glaze.

STRIPING—the addition of horizontal or vertical lines (or both) of any width.

STROKE ART PAINTING—a style of painting which uses individual brushstrokes to form subjects, often executed in a one-stroke approach with the application of color, value and form in one continuous movement.

TACKY—a sticky quality that develops during the drying time of a paint product.

THICK, CREAMY CONSISTENCY—a paint mixed with a very small amount of painting medium, paint glaze or solvent, whipped to the texture of whipped butter so that the paint holds peaks when patted with a palette knife.

THIN, CREAMY CONSISTENCY—a paint mixed with painting medium, paint glaze or solvent to the texture of whipped cream.

TONAL GRADATION—the creation of various color tones that intermingle and go down the gray scale in an even transition.

TONE ON TONE—the layering of two or more color values that are very similar in lightness or darkness.

TRANSPARENT—a coating of paint or glaze so thin that light can easily pass through.

VALUE—the ratio or percentage of color that relates to the gray scale; the variations of a color from lightest to darkest.

VARNISH—a clear coating of a polyurethane, water- or oil-based product that protects the coated surface.

WASH—paint that is thinned with enough painting medium, paint glaze or solvent to maker it fluid and transparent.

WET SANDING—the smoothing of a surface with a fine, wet/dry style sandpaper, wet with water and soap; the application is completed in the finishing stage, removing any imperfections between coats of varnish.

SOURCES

The following companies are the manufacturers, mail-order suppliers, or facilities that offer instructional materials or seminars that may be of interest to you. Please write for further information. Include a self-addressed return envelope to ensure a response.

Below are resources for the specific materials used in the creation of the decorated cabinets and chests in this book:

BRUSHES
Silver Brush Limited
92 N. Main Street, Bldg. 18C
Windsor, NJ 08561
(609) 443-4900
(609) 443-4888 (Fax)

GLAZES, GLUES, & VARNISHES
Back Street, Inc.
3905 Steve Reynolds Blvd.
Norcross, GA 30093
(770) 381-7373
(770) 381-6424 (Fax)

PAINTS (PRIMA ARTIST'S ACRYLICS)
Martin/ F. Weber Co.
2727 Southampton Rd.
Philadelphia, PA 19154
(215) 677-5600
(215) 677-3336 (Fax)

TAPES
3M Consumer Products Group
P.O. Box 33053
St. Paul, MN 55133
(612) 733-1110

The following companies produce the unfinished cabinets and chests decorated in this book.

- Faux Fabric: Red Plaid Trunk
- Frottage: Fleur-de-Lis
- Marquetry: Wood Staining

Wayne's Woodenware
1913 State Rd. 150
Neenah, WI 54956
(414) 725-7986
(414) 725-9386 (Fax)

- Stroke Art Painting: Vines and Berries Trunk

Mountain Man Products
P.O. Box 6997
Eureka, CA 95502
(707) 443-9171

- Monochromatic Painting: Daisies

Bush's Smoky Mt. Wood Products
3556 Wilhite Rd.
Sevierville, TN 37876
(423) 453-4829
(423) 428-6237 (Fax)

- Verdigris Finish: Checks

Sechtem's Wood Products

533 Margaret St.
Russell, KS 67665
(913) 483-2912
(913) 483-2960 (Fax)

• Folk Art Painting: Landscape
Cabin Crafters
1225 W. First St.
P.O. Box 270
Nevada, IA 50201
(800) 669-3920
(515) 382-3106 (Fax)

• Folk Art Painting: Rooster
The Cutting Edge
P.O. Box 3000-402
Chino, CA 91708
(909) 464-0440

• Punched Wood: Quilted Design
Unique Woods
400 N. Bowen, No. 114
Arlington, TX 76012
(817) 795-9650

• Decorative Painting: Leaves
• Folk Art Painting: Fruits
Allen's Wood Crafts
3020 Dogwood Lane, Route 3
Sapulpa, OK 74066
(918) 224-8796
(918) 224-3208 (Fax)

• Folk Art Painting: Peasant Couple
Khoury, Inc.
2201 E. Industrial Dr.
P.O. Box 729
Iron Mountain, MI 49801
(800) 553-5446
(906) 774-8211 (Fax)

• Decorative Painting: Roses
Valhalla Designs
343 Twin Pines Dr.
Attleboro Industrial Park
Glendale, OR 97442
(541) 832-3260
(541) 832-2424 (Fax)

• Dimensional Stenciling: Teacups
Country Crafts by Dal
2190 Kachina Dr.
Prescott, AZ 86301
(520) 771-0916

• Decorative Painting: Baroque
Florals
Renovated piece of furniture—no source available.

SCHOOLS
The following are schools that specialize in the teaching of paint and faux finishes for the decoration of accessories, furniture and interiors:

American Academy of Decorative Finishes
14255 N. 79th St., Suite 10
Scottsdale, AZ 85260
(602) 991-8560
(602) 991-9779 (Fax)

Day Studio Workshop, Inc.
1504 Bryant St.
San Francisco, CA 94103
(415) 626-9300

Finishing School, Inc.
334 Main St.
Port Washington, NY 11050
(516) 767-6422
(516) 767-7406 (Fax)

PCM Studios
School of the Decorative Arts
731 Highland Ave. NE, Suite D
Atlanta, GA 30312
(404) 222-0348
E-mail: abjpcm@aol.com

INDEX